Biblical Catechetics after Vatican II

BIBLICAL CATECHETICS
AFTER VATICAN II

by

Reverend Charles W. Paris

Priest of the Diocese of Wilmington

The Liturgical Press
Collegeville, Minnesota

Nihil obstat: John Eidenschink, O.S.B., J.C.D., *Censor deputatus.*
Imprimatur: † George H. Speltz, D.D., Bishop of St. Cloud. August 17, 1970.

Dedicated to
"All who hold and teach the Catholic Faith
that comes to us from the Apostles."
　　　　　　　　　　—*Roman Canon*

Foreword

To produce a book about matters of Christian doctrine is to capture in a certain number of words a great many years of religious experiences. For me, it is to synthesize the lessons learned from innumerable teachers beginning at elementary and going into graduate schooling, countless sermons and lectures, years of book and periodical reading. Then, when the digest is completed, to express that knowledge in my own personal wording.

Therefore, the only claim I make to originality is in the choice of words and word arrangements that fill this book. I openly concede my indebtedness to the nameless many who gave me the knowledge without which I could not have assembled the words. If, perchance, one or another of these benefactors should identify a thought as his own, I trust Christian charity and generosity will overlook the failure to express my indebtedness by a specific credit.

I thank Bishop Thomas J. Mardaga, my Ordinary, for his permission to publish this book; Eleanor Bachman, Caroline Hughes, Audrey Natale for production work on the manuscript; Father James J. Hanley, my colleague, for creating the book's title; James J. Ahern for professional services; the editorial and technical staff of The Liturgical Press for invaluable guidance and assistance.

For those who would wish a fuller and more systematic development of the points of Catholic faith which this book touches upon, I suggest a perusal of my former work, *The What and Why of Catholicism*.

Contents

Biblical Catechetics after Vatican II

CHAPTER I

The Bible

Ours is an age which looks upon contemporary conquests in the field of knowledge even while gazing forward to broader informational horizons. By science and technology modern ingenuity is "transforming the face of the earth," modifying long-established social, moral, and religious forms.

Because true knowledge and progress should develop man into the fullness of religious as well as human values, Vatican Council II in many of its documents called attention to the need and urgency of Christian education keeping abreast of its secular counterpart. The forward progress of man in secular knowledge, the Council Fathers noted, must not be alienated from religious values, nor should deeper insights and better understanding in the former leave the latter in a position of unimportance or irrelevancy. For religion to hold its proper place and role in the life of the twentieth—soon to be twenty-first—century, man rightly asks to meet God in terms intelligible to his own times and circumstances.

It is hardly valid to claim that because a prior system of catechetics produced satisfactory results—and it did, as the millions of today's deeply religious adult Christians amply testify—no changes should be made in it. The world outlook, the mid-century mind, customs, and norms have changed, and with that change a formerly successful methodology can be a less than effectual exercise today.

Hence religious instruction is donning a new garment—styling itself to the times and minds of today's peoples. This new attire has been designed by experimentation, fitted in the try-and-learn efforts of pioneer catechists, and given the status of acceptance in documents of an ecumenical council. Textbooks now reflect the new view, methodology utilizes it. The teacher or student who will be in step with the religious parade of our times must model upon it.

Yet this modern catechesis cannot, regardless of the intensity of the temptation, go beyond those limits which must, by the very nature of things, govern the principles of religion and religious education. The perspective of the "new approach" must be guided by some very old and fundamental concepts which have constantly been the base of Christian belief, lest the expenditure of energy and resources in new directions serve merely natural ends. Basic to the whole attitude toward religion and its proclamation is the truth that God is uncreated and pre-eminent, man is created and dependent; their relationship is not a mutuality of equals but a benevolence on the part of a superior and a gratitude on the part of an inferior. In a word, man is to be molded into God, not God adapted to man. Even while religion humanizes divinity, it is divinizing humanity, for the role of religion is not to limit the infinite but to expand the finite.

The challenge thus presented by a "new catechetics" is not to a theology which creates a new God or a psychology which produces a new man; rather, the methodology by which the traditional God is made known to contemporary man must be fitted to the modern man's concerns and experiences as found in his everyday living.

The unique fact of God and man becoming one in the historical figure of Jesus is (as it always has been in Christian tradition), the empirical substantiation that the true God and the whole man need not—indeed, must not—be detached concepts. The Incarnational Union exalted human nature beyond imagination. In the resurrection of the Incarnate Word, this same humanity was destined to a vista of eternal glorification which ever since has been the base and the summit of Christian doctrine, the vitalizing force of man's existence.

That one dazzling moment in history in which fallen human nature was uplifted by the Incarnation and glorified by the Resurrection has cast its radiance backward and forward throughout the reaches of history. Every historical human event is colored bright or dark by virtue of its conformity to or divergence from Jesus, the perfect union of God and man: brightened insofar as conformity to Him is had, darkened to the extent He is not reflected in it. Seen in the perspective of the Risen Jesus, the invitation from God to man and the response of man to God comes into clearer view in every period of humanity's presence in world history.

God speaks to man in manifold ways: human reason contacts divinity, as did the philosophers; nature itself teaches us about Him, as St. Paul noted; the Bible records His word, as orthodox faith has consistently maintained; the Catholic Church, teacher of faith and morals, is acknowledged by millions as the living, authoritative voice of revelation. But singularly and uniquely, Jesus communicated God to man because He Himself was truly God; Jesus best received God on behalf of man because Jesus was Himself true man. Reason, nature, Bible, Church are all centered in and emanate from the historical fact that the one, natural Son of God was made flesh, lived, died, and arose from death unto everlasting life. Religious content and religion's methodology can be valuable to mankind to its fullest extent only insofar as the central position of this risen Jesus is the primary point of doctrine and conduct. Religion must be the medium of communication of God with man and man's response to God's message—in and through Jesus.

The most codified and universally acceptable record of this communication, and motivator of fitting response, is the Bible. A new and effective modern-day approach to religion's divine-human dialogue is therefore being sought in a more ready acceptance and deeper understanding of Sacred Scripture in religious learning and teaching. As Vatican Council II noted, the books of the Bible are really God's books, because, "Written under the inspiration of the Holy Spirit . . . they have God as their author . . . ." They are the Church's books, for "the task of authentically interpreting the word of God . . . has been entrusted exclusively to the living teaching office of the Church." It is basic, then, that an approach to a new catechesis rests upon the textbook par excellence, the Bible, and that some basic facts regarding this book be recalled. The Bible is truly many books in that it embraces the works of many contributors, writers, and editors; it spans many centuries in time of composition, and it uses many different literary forms for conveying its message. Yet, these many books are really but one book because of one principal author, God, and one overriding theme, an unfolding of God's involvement in the affairs of men and of man's reaction to that divine intervention.

The Bible, basically, is a two-part book: the Old Testament and the New Testament, with Jesus centrally located at the convergence of the two. The first part of the book looks forward to the coming of the Messiah upon the historical scene, which was fulfilled in the person of Jesus; the second part looks back upon Him, and through the light of His resurrected glory, to His coming again. Yet, even while looking back and looking forward, He remains, through the life-application of the biblical teaching, a here-and-now dynamic force for individual people and for the community of God's People.

The exact date of the writing of any given book of the Bible and the exact human author of many of the books are matters of scholarly debate. There are no extant, original manuscripts of the biblical books as such. It is a solid opinion among Scripture scholars that many of the biblical books are the products of contributions from many writers and various oral traditions, likely brought into the now accepted and recognized form by final editors.

Accepted standards put the composition of the Old Testament books as now constituted within the period of the last six centuries of the Old Testament era. The New Testament books appeared approximately between the years of 40 and 100 of the Christian epoch. Thus the total span of time for the formulation of the biblical books as we now have them is some seven centuries.

The constant practice of Christian tradition has included the Old Testament books as part of its biblical heritage, a stand reiterated and endorsed by Vatican Council II: "The plan of salvation . . . is found as the true word of God in the books of the Old Testament . . . these books therefore . . . remain permanently valuable." In the course of Jewish tradition this ancient heritage, however, came to exist in two forms; this occasioned a problem for primitive Christianity.

After the fall of Jerusalem in 70 A.D., rabbinic scholars compiled a listing of their sacred writings that in time became known as the Palestinian (or Protocanonical) canon. For centuries prior to that time, a collection of books called the Septuagint (a Greek word for "seventy," chosen because of the tradition that seventy scholars made the Greek translation and compilation) had been in use by Jews living to some extent in Palestine but principally in Egypt and Greek-speaking areas. The Septuagint Scripture contained seven books and several passages from other books which did not appear in the later Palestinian edition; this additional material became known as "deuterocanonical."

Some uncertainty was present in the early Christian community, and remained through centuries of discussion, as to which of these two canons should be accepted as authentic. A full consideration of this point is presently afield of our subject; suffice it to say that usage and repeated official and unofficial expressions of faith warranted the solemn pronouncement of the Septuagint canon as containing the divinely inspired books of the Old Testament. During the chaotic period of the sixteenth century, however, Protestantism chose for its Bible the Palestinian canon. Hence, Catholic editions of the Bible have books and verses in the Old Testament section which are not found in Protestant Bibles.

The Old Testament of the Catholic Bible contains forty-six books, which allow for broad identification as: twenty-one historical/legal books, eighteen books of the prophets, seven books of wisdom literature.

In substance, the historical/legal books record events and personages which figured prominently in the emergence of the nation and its continuing relationship with God and neighboring countries. In these books are recorded the laws under which the nation would maintain its covenant relationship with Yahweh.

In the books of the prophets, these divinely chosen and enlightened men reiterated the terms of the contract which existed between God and the nation by virtue of which the Israelites were Yahweh's Chosen People. In the light of this divine-human covenant, the prophets called Israel from lapses into false ways back to the true service of God. In their writings, the prophets added to the unfolding picture of the Messiah-to-come.

The wisdom literature captured the admonitions of the sages for living the personally good life of this earth while preparing for the glory of the next—trying to give, in the light of heavenly values, some workable answers to life's many vexations.

The New Testament comprises twenty-seven books. Four recount the good news of the coming of the Messiah. This gospel is of two types: three versions featuring events in the life of Christ and referred to as the "Synoptic Gospel" (because a common record of events runs through them), and attributed to the authorship of the Apostle Matthew and the latter disciples Mark and Luke; one version, more interpretative and doctrinal (an editorializing upon the events in Jesus' life, pointing out particularly the divine aspect of His messianic role), which is credited to the authorship of the Apostle John.

The other books of the New Testament are The Acts of the Apostles, a history of the first days of the Church considered written by the disciple Luke, and twenty-one letters (epistles) to various Christian communities (or persons) which propound Gospel doctrine in one way or another; the majority of these writings are attributed to the Apostle Paul, with others credited to the Apostles James, Peter, John, and Jude. Lastly there is one book of eschatological prophecy believed to have been written by the Apostle John.

The original source material of both the Old and New Testaments was oral tradition. In the case of the Old Testament, a small part of that tradition went back to the obscurity of Israel's prehistory. From this beginning and down through centuries of development, individuals on the move met others so engaged; families associated with each other and clans were formed; clans discovered the advantages of federation and the nation was born. Throughout this process a person-to-person and a generation-to-generation handing on of happenings and impressions gradually developed a lore that became a history. From the word of mouth accounts of roving nomads, from the memories the older generation passed to the younger as both were gathered around the campfire of a tent village, a highly perfected power of narration and retention developed, and was considered a very important part of a continuing human existence. In the course of time written records were made and the oral traditions of the past were able to be preserved in the more stable form of documents.

In stark contrast the New Testament existed in oral tradition less than twenty years before its first book (First Thessalonians) was composed. Moreover, its cultural milieu was far advanced from the primitive style of the Old Testament counterpart. The Christian Church was an already well-organized and operating reality before any book of its own proper Scripture was written. And when these words were set down, they captured the spoken word which was taught and preached by the Apostles and other eyewitnesses of Jesus' life and works, as well as information and recollections which one witness would hand on to another in the community of the Church.

It ought to be noted that the use of the terms oral tradition and written word does not constitute a dual source of religious knowledge but rather two facets of one source—God. In the pre-Christian era God spoke through the writers of the sacred books as they utilized the accumulated experiences God's people encountered in living out the divine plan. In Jesus, God Himself spoke as the Divine Wisdom Incarnate. This message was penned by chosen authors so that it would be preserved for the generations to come. The source of revelation is God Himself; the expression of this revelation is oral tradition and written word. "Hence there exist a close connection and communication between sacred tradition and Sacred Scripture. For both of them, flowing from the same divine wellspring, in a certain way merge into a unity and tend toward the same end" (Vatican II).

To this duality must be added also the official teaching function of the Church as it interprets and explains the content and meaning of revelation for the peoples of all times. "It is clear, therefore, that sacred tradition, Sacred Scripture and the teaching authority of the Church in accord with God's most wise design, are so linked and joined together that one cannot stand without the others, and that all together and each in its own way under the action of the one Holy Spirit contribute effectively to the salvation of souls" (Vatican II).

Before the Bible, as such, emerged, a choosing and sifting process was necessary. As can be imagined, the scope of the oral and written material of the Old and New Testament historical periods was quite immense. Indeed, within this tremendous body of religious teaching there were accounts which varied and some which conflicted. It was imperative that authoritative decisions be forthcoming as to what constituted the authentic word of God to His people.

We have already noted how steps taken in this direction resulted in the emergence and use of the Septuagint and Palestinian canons of the Old Testament.

As the Christian Church developed its posture in the world community, it was faced with the task of sorting out from its own body of Christian writings that which could bear the label of God's authoritative word. In addition, the Christian assembly needed also to set its seal of approval upon one of the two current editions of the Old Testament.

This monumental task of deciding the canon of the Bible was undertaken by many scholars and Church leaders. Milestone dates in the process occurred during the second century with the translation of the First Latin version, at Hippo in North Africa in 393 A.D., at Carthage in North Africa in 397 A.D. and 418 A.D., and at Trent on April 8, 1546, when the matter was solemnly and definitively formalized as part of revealed Catholic faith. To question the divinely inspired character of the Catholic canon after that date is tantamount to heresy. Strictly speaking, divine inspiration is true only of the original compositions—in Hebrew, Aramaic, Greek. Translations into the vernacular serve as vehicles to bring the message of the inspired original to peoples of countless languages.

Once the authoritative text of the Bible was established, its perpetuation was a herculean task. In the absence of volume printing devices, the only method of reproduction was by handmade transcriptions. Mostly this work was done by monks who gave their whole lifetime to this arduous but sacred task. Not only did these dedicated copyists preserve the Bible for posterity by their labor, but because it was considered so holy a production, they embellished its pages with artistic designs and colors. These ancient manuscripts rank high among the art treasures of mankind.

With the advent of printing in the fifteenth century, copies of the Bible in many languages were produced by the new technique. Catholic sources had produced over six hundred printed editions of the Bible before the Protestant versions began to appear. The Catholic Bible in English, the Douay-Rheims, was issued in 1582 A.D., twenty-nine years before the King James (Protestant) edition.

The immediacy and frequency of printed editions of the Bible verifies the Church's continuing interest in placing God's holy word in the hands and minds of the faithful. Indeed, in the older days of the handmade Scripture, which took, perhaps, a lifetime of human labor to produce, the monetary value of the holy book was inestimable. To prevent theft of these texts, so that their content and use would be available to the people, great precautions were exercised in guarding the holy books, and their existence was largely confined to churches and monasteries. But once the printing process made large volume and low cost possible, the distribution of the Bible was no longer limited to a church or monastery but could be extended to private homes.

The Bible has been, in whole and in part, among the most treasured of human possessions for an almost unimaginably long time. As such it has been the subject of very intensive analysis and study. Yet, it is quite safe to claim that its cultural or historical context (if not its religious message) has been more precisely investigated in the last one hundred years than in all the accumulated centuries which went before. This scholarship has richly rewarded mankind in its appreciation of biblical background as well as of the word of God.

To substantiate this claim, we must realize the great contribution which science has made, by its breakthroughs, to all other areas of human knowledge and understanding.

The science of archeology has uncovered many of the places wherein the biblical narrative was enacted, and by its findings in these ruins has verified events and details which authenticated parallel Scriptural assertions. This same science has brought to light household and other articles whereby the life and culture of Scriptural times could be better grasped. It has recovered writings made by other than the biblical authors and other than the Israelite or early Christian peoples, thereby providing contemporary and disinterested authorities with which to compare the Scripture writings.

Linguistics has contributed its share by learning how to decipher ancient writings so that they are intelligible to our own manner of expression, and to uncover precise shades of meaning the ancient words and idioms—both Old and New Testament—had in the times and cultures in which they were commonly used, hence in the meaning they had when employed in Scriptural writings.

Geology has contributed its share to verification of biblical assertions by more precisely investigating and interpreting characteristics of the earth's composition so that biblical statements could be verified or be put in a more accurate perspective.

Historians have widely expanded their knowledge of peoples whose nations and cultures have long since passed from the active scene. A greater knowledge of people and civilizations other than the Israelite nation itself or of the contemporaries of Jesus' time gives a standard against which to check and a source from which to verify.

The advance of human knowledge into the field of radioactivity has not been without benefit to Scriptural research, for many of this science's discoveries and techniques have contributed to a more specific determination of the age of ancient documents and increased the reliability of judgment as to their authenticity, integrity, and value.

Even the computer has been put to good service as a tool of Scriptural investigation as documents are studied for those characteristics which will better identify originality and authorship.

Catholic Scripture scholars armed with such corroborative evidence and encouraged by Papal directives are able to enter into the very times and mentality of the people, culture, and theology of the Bible and more accurately to evaluate in the norms of the then contemporary living environment the substance of what God's written word is intended to convey.

Advances in biblical scholarship and in scientific investigation have combined to give today's Bible reader and student a more accurate and meaningful understanding of the divine message of the Bible and of the literary forms used by its human authors.

Even such a summary view of the Bible as has preceded, indicates the breadth and complexity which might be expected within its pages. This one book offers practical and speculative history, science, law, theology, prophecy, and wisdom.

These many fields are presented in differing literary forms among which figures of speech, legends, parables, prayers, poetry, and sermons are clearly discernible. Yet the Bible cannot be considered as a history, law, or science book in the present-day sense of these terms; nor can its variety of authors, forms of expression, or time span in composition relegate it to a mere conglomeration of random writings. Rather, the variety of content and form found in the Bible serves a central purpose: to convey the biblical message, namely, to make God known to man, and to make known the sin/grace relationship of man to God in terms of historical existence. The Bible is not merely a source to learn "about" God, but *a means for sinful man to meet God.* This is the Bible's reason-for-being. If it is not for this moral purpose that man uses it, then why have a Bible at all?

The Bible is concerned with a real God, real people, real life situations. This explains why its passages are sometimes lofty, sometimes on the seamy side. It is an account of life as it really is.

Proper understanding of the biblical message supposes some grasp of the styles used by the human author in setting down his ideas. In this area, it is useful to make a distinction between the precise message God intends the Bible to communicate to man and the written container by means of which the human author conveys that message.

Oftentimes a container gives some knowledge of contents —a paper bag indicates that the product contained within it is not liquid or gas. But also, there is a real difference between the container and what it contains. This is also true to an extent of the Bible and a valid guide in biblical understanding. The message of salvation is the essential content of the Bible; the various forms of writing style found in this book constitute the container. Many times a knowledge of the container leads to a better knowledge of the content. From one aspect, it might be said that the content (divine message) is primarily the area of doctrinal teaching; the container (form of writing) is the realm of investigation and interpretation. In no instance does the container contain a message distinct from or independent of the divine message proper to the text under consideration. Medium and message are always one.

We have already indicated various literary forms used in the Bible, such as law, prophecy, wisdom, parable, poem, sermon, etc. It is of first importance in grasping the message being conveyed to understand the form being used and the impact upon the message that form might have. As a simple example: what appears to be a recording of a historical event could actually be a fable or a piece of biography or a parable; words given an expressed poetic form will be interpreted differently from the same words set in prose form. Depending on which form the author intended, the interpretation placed upon his words can vary.

This necessity to grasp the implications inherent in the literary form itself has led to a study known as "Form Criticism." According to the norms of this discipline, the text itself, the words within a text, the context, the language, the author's sources, the reason for choosing a particular literary form, the true author, the time and environment of the original writing are some of the points of investigation. In the light of the long period of time the Scriptural books have been in existence and the many copies made by individual scribes, Form Criticism provides invaluable service in distinguishing original material from variants which have crept in over the centuries, as well as in setting a particular book or detail in an overall perspective.

Clearer understanding of Scriptural forms, linguistic nuances, and initial cultural environment certainly enables one to grasp the divine message in more authentic dimensions. There will be, correspondingly, a difference of accent and an adjustment of interpretation of the Scripture from one time era to another and on varying levels of scholarship. It is therefore valid to say that the sacred writings have an aspect of existential permanence and meaning.

But this admission is not to be understood as excluding an essential, eternal verity to the biblical writing. In other words, the truth contained in the innumerable formal judgments of Sacred Scripture is immutable and extends to all men always. One destroys the nature of Scripture if its divine message is made only as enduring as a given temporal or cultural period. The divinely inspired and guaranteed teaching of a former age cannot be different from what it is in a present period or what it will be in time to come, for to posit such a possibility regarding the Bible message would destroy it as the authentic word of God; and in that destruction God would be destroyed because the Bible, being God's own book, would record God as contradicting Himself.

It is therefore important to bear in mind throughout any exploration of the Bible as the message of God, and in particular in the sometimes very confusing areas of container-content, literary forms, form criticism, and textual interpretation, that the divinely guided teaching office of the Church is the ordinary and final arbiter for Christian catechesis. When the variety of literary forms, the diversity of linguistic usages, the variance in cultures of the human authors and their immediate audiences, the profundity of the subject matter, the divergent backgrounds and various philosophical premises of exegetes—when all of these factors are weighed in the balance, it seems self-evident that determination of the true meaning of a text requires more than a mere human skill or learning. Only the Church can officially and publicly supply this higher requisite.

This anchoring upon a substantive teaching authority is particularly valuable when new insights or erroneous deductions may argue to positions radically contrary to accepted beliefs, as, for example, when some biblical event is uncovered as an illustration rather than an historical fact. If the item thus reappraised is some well-known and widely accepted concept, to suggest that it never really happened but actually was the original author's descriptive tool for better expressing an idea is rather upsetting to the non-scholar. Good sense should govern both the teacher and the taught. The scholar is putting forth (if he is a reputable scholar) a theory he considers well grounded; but he was not an eyewitness. Even if his theory is true and the supposed "event" was merely an "illustration," it does not affect the Bible's authenticity—it is the content of the passage that is the object of faith, not the academic debate about the stylistic device in which the message came. The teaching Church must have the final say upon the matter.

In the light of what has been written here about the human and temporal influences upon God's book, precisely in what sense can it be said that God is its primary author? The answer to this query brings us to two most difficult biblical questions: "What is inspiration?" "What is inerrancy?" Too often scholars have forgotten that these propositions are in the realm of faith; and all items of faith involve mystery. Mystery means that we have absolute certainty in certain respects, partial understanding in some respects, and ignorance in still other respects. When God reveals a truth he never reveals answers to all the questions that man may think up.

Vatican Council II, in directing itself to the subject of Scriptural inspiration, states, "Those divinely revealed realities which are contained and presented in Sacred Scripture have been committed to writing under the inspiration of the Holy Spirit. Holy Mother Church . . . holds that the books of both the Old and New Testament in their entirety . . . have God as their author . . . ." Relative to the human authors, the Council states, "In composing the sacred books, God chose men and while employed by Him, they made use of their powers and abilities so that with Him acting in them and through them they, as true authors, consigned to writing everything and only those things which He wanted . . . The books of Scripture must be acknowledged as teaching solidly, faithfully, and without error that truth which God wanted put into the sacred writings for the sake of our salvation."

Inspiration of the Bible, then, can be described as the special grace of God whereby the Holy Spirit moved the human authors of the Bible books to record everything and only those things which God wanted written into this sacred record, and to do this in a form natural to the human author. Inspiration must touch every formal judgment; otherwise statements not so touched would not be from God, would not be part of the Bible. Inspiration cannot be limited to matters of faith and morality or to such items as more evidently affect our salvation. The forms or ways in which statements are made are multiple; judgments must be distinguished from the way or manner in which they are expressed.

Detecting and isolating the precise character of the formal judgment at times is very difficult, especially when the method of expression involves figurative language, sense perception versus scientific objectivity or one of the many, many different types of history. Statements touching the world of nature or the course of history in the Bible are no less inspired than statements on the nature of God.

How did God accomplish this inspiration? That is another complex question. Certainly not in the sense that a writer holds a pen and moves it to write, for the human author was a truly free agent (grace does not destroy nature). Perhaps more likely (and this analogy is admittedly limping), as a simultaneous translator (such as is used at the U.N.), who expresses the thoughts of another while yet freely choosing his own words and expressions.

As to the inerrancy or, better, the truth of the biblical writings, it follows from the preceding analysis of inspiration and the quotations of the Council that the Bible's freedom from error is *not* in the sense of this whole book as a religious work—leaving chapters and verses subject to error whenever a spiritual message is not readily evident. It is most logical that if what is written is everything and only what God wanted written, then the entire God-intended content—every formal judgment—is beyond error. Upon the exegete falls the heavy and oftentimes extremely difficult task of ascertaining what is actually "being taught"; the "vehicle for the teaching" has no existence in itself and therefore presents no grounds for error or truth.

Enough has been said that the conclusion should be inevitable: the Bible is the most extraordinary book! Its origin, its development, its endurance challenge human comprehension. Yet, the greatest mystery of the Bible is that it is truly a form of God's presence on earth, in time, and among His people.

Religious people have grown accustomed to the idea of God's presence everywhere in all of creation—His *omnipresence*. Catholics have the greatest belief in His presence in sanctifying grace and in the sacrament of the Holy Eucharist. Perhaps the idea is not so common, but it is no less true, that God exerts a special form of "omnipresence" in the words of the Bible. Vatican Council II, in its decree on the liturgy, stated that "[Jesus] is really present in His word, since it is He Himself who speaks from the holy Scriptures that are read in the Church." This concept must be grasped, realized, and made a part of religious living. Respect for the book as such, respect for the message of life which it contains, respect for the response it calls upon man to make—these all must be actuated in and from the knowledge that where God's word is, there, too, is God. "Through this revelation, therefore, the invisible God out of the abundance of His love speaks to men as friends and lives among them" (Vatican II).

Because of the exalted nature of the Bible, it enters into the liturgical life of God's people, communicating His word to them, nourishing them by His truth, and evoking from them a response of loving submission. The place of Sacred Scripture in the life of worship is not accidental or incidental but essential and vital, and this necessity must be grasped, accepted, and utilized to the fullest benefit of all, ". . . since from the table of both the word of God and of the body of Christ, [the Church] unceasingly receives and offers to the faithful the bread of life, especially in the sacred liturgy" (Vatican II).

*   *   *   *   *

The lesson which the Bible presents is that of salvation history—the narration of God's involvement in the affairs of man and man's response to that divine intervention. Preeminently, because Jesus is the hinge between the two Testa-

ments and the apex of the epic story, salvation history nar-
rates God's acting in the Incarnation-Redemption mystery from
its temporal beginning at creation until its consummation at
the parousia. Salvation history records God and man journeying
together in Jesus, the Lord of History, through time—from the
eternity which gave it birth to the same eternity which shall
receive it at death.

In this saga, as in any history, appear the great names of
the heroes—Abraham, Moses, John the Baptist, Mary, Peter,
Augustine, and many more. Around these personages were
the innumerable "little people," unknown and unsung. But
without their contribution to the continuing march of events,
the central figures would never have emerged, the history
never have occurred.

But in salvation history, unlike its secular counterpart,
the unknown person is not relegated to unending oblivion.
Secular history passes and its events die; but salvation history
looks ahead to a life renewed in and with the glorified Jesus.
Then the "little man" will be exalted, and his exaltation will
be eternal. For every human response—to or against the invitation from God—is remembered for its part in accomplishing
the goal toward which salvation history inexorably moves.

In the broad expanse which is salvation history, then,
the Old Testament would be unfinished without Jesus to fulfill it; the New Testament likewise would be incomplete without His final proclamation of the ultimate triumph of God.
The figure of Jesus as Messiah so totally impregnates and
dominates every scene and facet of salvation history that the
subject would be non-existent without Him. Neither the
Bible nor a catechetics based upon it will have meaning or
be effective unless this centrality of Jesus—Incarnate, Sacrificed, Resurrected—is clearly grasped and convincingly presented. Indeed, He is the Prophet, the Priest, the King!

CHAPTER II

The Faith

Faith is a standard tool in the workshop of man's progress. The faith of a scientist or engineer in the truth of some theory pushes him to continue searching for ways and means to bring his ideas into concrete reality. Faith in the possibility of human improvement in fellow man and in secular institutions motivates men to give their life labor for intangible rewards rather than material benefits. Faith establishes and perpetuates parent-child, husband-wife, teacher-student, physician-patient, lawyer-client and many other relationships without which humane living would be impossible. Indeed, faith is a more predominant characteristic of man's natural life than any other of his attributes.

Yet, some men find the ascent from dependence on natural faith to belief in supernatural faith most difficult or totally impossible. Religious education, as an appeal to supernatural faith, must face this barrier. The task of catechetics is to prepare non-receptive minds for the acceptance of religious truths (the actual bestowal of supernatural faith is by God, as a gift), as well as to intensify religious faith in those in whom it has already been divinely planted.

Both natural and supernatural faith are forms of knowledge. Whereas "to know" is the effect of experienced phenomena, a sense apprehension which leads to certitude and is subject to empirical proof, "to believe" is acceptance on authority, an intellectual apprehension which concludes to conviction beyond reasonable doubt but is incapable of full demonstration. Many of the difficulties in making supernatural faith convincing lie in a failure to make the distinction between "to know" and "to believe" and to be bound by the difference. Supernatural faith too often is called upon to carry a heavier load of "proof" than its nature allows; when it collapses under the overburden, the result is a discrediting of the entire realm of the supernatural.

Science, mostly, can place its principles under the microscope of laboratory procedures and verify itself by sensory apprehension. Religion cannot do this, and to attempt such a feat leads only to frustration at the least and disaster at the most.

Rather, the principles of religion are presented in the realm of intellectual persuasion—dependence on the intellect to fulfill its natural function, namely, to accede to truth. The solidity of a premise and the logic of its development should induce reason to conclude to the validity of the conclusion. If the premise, development, and conclusion fulfill their true specification yet the intellect refuses to accept the argumentation, the refusal then is unreasonable—against reason—and faith can offer no further motivation of its own. This is simply an unwarranted refusal, a rejection of knowledge on the part of the rejecter.

Affirmation of the truth or falsity (the "believability") of a judgment rests upon the evidence sustaining it. Lack or insufficiency of evidence places the intellect in a state of doubt; due evidence moves the intellect to accept the proposition as true or reject it as false. When the evidence is compelling enough to call for a true or false judgment but the intellect remains in doubt or chooses to make its affirmation in opposition to the true or false value of the evidence, the operation of that intellect is unreasonable. The conclusiveness of a proposition of religion and the affirmation of faith require valid premises, deductions, and conclusions and an intellect operating properly and honestly. Logically, then, the intellect ought to accept the proposal as a truth if the evidence is in favor of truth or as a falsity if the evidence weighs in that direction.

Phenomena able to be experienced in an empirical fashion are their own proof of truth, for they are sense-apprehended and therefore subject to doubt-free certitude. All other knowledge man must accept on authority to the degree that conviction overpowers doubt—and this is *faith*. Obviously, then, the major part of human knowledge is in the order of faith: natural faith for natural things, supernatural faith for the things of an order above the earthly—principally the order of religion.

The amount of conviction sustaining both natural and supernatural faith depends on the integrity of the authority which proposes and vouches for the item to be believed. The more responsible and informed the authority, the more credence should be put in the proposition. The things believed by mankind in the worldly order rest on human authority; the things proposed for man's belief in the authentic supernatural order rest upon God's authority. Because of God's total knowledge and His total integrity, it ought to be self-evident that faith in matters supernatural is more solidly founded than faith in purely natural things.

What actually constitutes this body of authentic revelation emanating from and resting upon divine authority will be most safely ascertained, as has been noted in the previous chapter, from the Bible, tradition, and the teaching, interpreting Church. In these three are expressed the fullness of God's outpouring in the person of the revealing Jesus. Because supernatural faith is based upon authority and will be defensible only to the extent authority is sustained, it is of paramount importance that religious presentation rest on an authoritative foundation, that is, the true biblical message, the accepted and recognized tradition, and the Church teaching. The teaching Church, it must be noted, is the Supreme Pontiff, the college of bishops, or both, for the universal Church, the local bishop for his diocese. Theologians, respected and necessary though they are, are but adjuncts to the teaching Church, often speculators and theorists about the content, extent, and application of the deposit of faith. Theologians present theories, the teaching Church presents facts.

But experience, as has already been mentioned, amply demonstrates that religious faith, though resting on the higher authority of God, is not as universally accepted as is secular faith, which is based on merely human authority. Several factors explain this illogical state of affairs.

Underlying all other reasons and therefore first in the order of importance is the egotism which is inherent in mankind. Man's nature is highly endowed, for he is made in the image of God. But this noble estate too often twists man's sense of values to the point where he conceives of himself as actually being a god. Rather than possessing the humility of accepting the lesser status of a reflection, man asserts a claim to be the original itself. Because human nature possesses an appetite for the infinite, it sometimes confuses humans about their finiteness. It is interesting to note that the Genesis writer records this vulnerable point, identifying it as the grounds for the first temptation to disbelief, ". . . you shall be as gods. . . ."

Other obstacles to supernatural faith for the modern unbeliever, or even to a fullness of it for many believers, can be found within and without man. Singly or in various combinations and in varying degrees, some of the more prominent causes follow.

Man's own reasoning power often leads him away from God's word rather than to it. For example, day-to-day life events give many examples of violated trusts: marriage infidelity reflected in adultery or divorce; parental disinterest and neglect in relation to the behavior of offspring; politics as "the art of the possible" in preference to statesmanship for the good of society; capital-labor mutual exploitation and disregard by both for the common welfare; public figures such as physicians, policemen, clergymen exposed in practices inimical to their public image.

But religion is built on trust—trust in God's goodness, mercy, justice. If man finds his fellowman engaged in life-practices destructive of and belying trust, he becomes skeptical about putting his own trust in God and the promises of religion.

Modern environment provides difficulties to a full assent to the higher faith. Our era places great value upon personal independence, initiative, creativity; rebellion against the concept and strictures of organization and even of society itself (especially among the younger generation) is used as a manifestation of authenticity and integrity. But supernatural faith demands a discipline of intellect and will in calling for dependence on God and Church, a subscription to orthodoxy, a submission to authority within a structured establishment. Religion thus seems opposed to the values by which man governs his natural pursuits.

The accepted philosophy of modern times conditions man to resist the logic of religious faith. The pragmatism of today which identifies the true and the good with practicality—"if it works it is true and good"—makes man skeptical of religious ideals viewed against the background of his daily experiences. Unprincipled personal behavior, organized violence, social injustice as a way of life are but a few of the realities man garners from observation of the scene around him and perusal of the daily newspaper. Religion's appeal to behavior reflecting self-discipline, fraternal love, honesty and the other virtues seems untrue and inexpedient when it fails to "work" among flesh and blood acquaintances.

Man's technological advancements transfer many of the prerogatives once reserved to the divine province to a realm within human power. The manufacture and orbiting of space modules, the supplying of fertility to the soil, the production of new mineral elements and the radical changing of others, man-made fibres and the like which replace natural counterparts, compounding of "miracle" drugs and invention of replacements for bodily organs, the regulation of life by fertilizing the sterile or nullifying the fertile—all such marvelous advancements whet the appetite for more (and more come forth almost daily). Will not scientific discovery and technological expertise eventually bring the day when divinity can be relegated to the obsolete?

The violation of trust, the environment of personal emancipation, the prevalence of pragmatic judgments, the accelerated pace of human achievement in the fields of science and technology are but a few of the counterforces to a full and free acceptance of supernatural faith against which the case for religious truths competes. It must be admitted that superficial considerations give such arguments a semblance of credibility. There is one more objection to religious truth, however, and this is so totally illogical that its appeal to intelligent persons challenges explanation. Yet an appeal it has!

Supernatural faith proposes for acceptance certain propositions which are beyond the power of the human intellect to understand fully. These proposals are referred to as "mysteries." Because religious truth and morality very definitely include mysteries, some would reject supernatural faith as being unintellectual.

Such reasoning is strange indeed. Man himself and the world he lives in abound in things not fully understood but readily admitted and accepted as real. In the natural order few people have any understanding of the inner nature of electricity, hurricanes, or atomic energy; scientific phenomena such as TV, computers, or chemical alteration and rearrangement of molecular structures are areas of ignorance for most of the people whose daily lives are vitally influenced by them. The physiological processes of digestion and nutrition, diversity of bodily end products from a common nutritional material, the origin, continuation, and termination of bodily life—all propose such profound questions that scholars seeking answers merely scratch the surface even after a lifetime of specialized investigation. The psychological differentiation whereby man specifically distinguishes himself from the animal—knowledge of language, of ends and alternate means to accomplish ends, the power of choice and of invention, the unduplicated multiplication of personality, the attraction and endurance of one human's love for another—all and many more are taken for granted by every man as due qualities of his nature, yet they are understood in their true depth and fullness by no man.

It is noteworthy to realize that even the few examples of natural mysteries just cited fall into the same created, finite order of existence as man himself. Since man cannot comprehend even his own order of being, is it not quite incongruous for him to reject an order of existence infinitely superior to his own, simply on the basis of his inability fully to comprehend its every detail? Should man, who can accept the understandability gap between himself and his pet dog (a very finite separation), find it inconsistent that there be a difficulty in comprehension of the infinite difference between himself and God?

From the preceding comments, a natural mystery can be defined as "a reality whose existence is known but which the human intellect cannot fully comprehend."

A supernatural mystery—as encountered in religious doctrine—fits the same definition. The unity and trinity of God, the union of divine and human natures in the one Person of Jesus, the efficacy of the sacraments in reproducing the God-life in a human soul, the living presence of Jesus in the sacrament of the Holy Eucharist, the Church as the Mystical Body of Jesus, the nature of sin and the relation of the natural law to the moral law are some of the religious propositions (mysteries) presented by religion for human belief. Each is a reality whose existence is known from revelation as it is investigated by human reason. Each is beyond the ability of the human intellect's capacity for full comprehension. Therefore, each is truly a mystery; but saying that is in no way to say that religious mysteries are unintellectual or that they should inhibit the assent of religious faith any more than the natural mysteries compel rejection of the incomprehensibles they offer to the human intellect.

Indeed, the existence of mysteries within religious doctrine argues to and confirms the validity and believability of religion. If man admits mysteries on his own level of reality (and he cannot deny them!), it seems normal and natural that a level of reality higher than the human should also have its mysteries. Right-thinking man should recognize from his way of living in the natural order that a religion in which every detail could be perfectly explained and grasped would be unreal and abnormal.

Returning to the previously mentioned reasons for the refusal of so many present-day persons to accept the religious beliefs proposed by supernatural faith, a little reflection on these claims demonstrates that the decision to reject religion because of them is ill-founded and erroneous:

The violation of trust, so much a part of daily living, is attributable in a great measure to man's refusal to believe in the "brotherhood of man in the Fatherhood of God," which is a basic principle of the Christian religion. No sounder foundation exists for mutual confidence among men than a bond of unity stemming from a common source.

The environment of personal emancipation can only be realized in terms of true adulthood and autonomy when individuals are free and mature enough to subject self-will and selfish ways to the good of the whole society, thereby making a personal contribution toward the dignity due every human being. Religion demands just such a true, mature, and educated commitment.

The prevalence of pragmatic judgments as a measuring standard can witness to the real "workability" of religious faith. Religion calls man to a life of dedication, higher cultural and social levels, fraternal concern and charity. If these are not the coin-of-exchange in the modern marketplace, it is because, on the whole, religious tenets have received lip service rather than application. Yet enough cases of people living truly religious lives and doing great good for others exist to show that "workability" and religion are highly compatible.

The accelerated pace of human achievement in the fields of science and technology will never replace divinity; these fields merely witness to God's eternal plan. Religion, as does science, builds on principles, systematic teaching, human psychology, and history; technological feats fulfill the commission given to mankind as the ruler of creation—"have dominion over the whole earth"— witnessing to a partnership between God and man rather than a divine-human competition: God creates, man uses that creation to invent.

The stress upon the "present" by modern education and society to the detriment of the two other time-dimensions of existence is also an influential cause eliciting an indifference toward religious beliefs among the faithless and even weakening religion's appeal to some professed believers, lay and clerical. This limited-outlook approach is seen, relative to the past, for example, in the indifference to history as an academic subject; and to the future, by mortgaging unborn generations to solve current political and sociological problems.

The present is a connecting link between past and future, not exclusively an entity in itself; the present has value because of its relationship to past and future. An exclusively here-and-now life objective ignores past history and traditions as well as the future's goals and benefits; it is pure expediency.

Supernatural faith calls for a three-dimensional temporal perspective on life and its activities—respect for and an influence from the past pages of salvation history, a present creedal affirmation exemplified within an ecclesial society, a future-looking life pattern directed beyond the partial goods of time to the ultimate good of eternity. In this demand, religion conforms itself to the realities of life and time and stands opposed to the illusion that past and future are of little or no meaning. For those fixated upon present existence only, the challenge presented to contemporary thought by a past-present-future synthesis is a barrier to real faith-commitment.

Supernatural faith was born in the Garden of Eden at the dawn of human existence. God asked mankind to trust in the divine judgment as to what was good and what was evil and, on the divine authority, to forego the evil. In return for giving up something of his own dominion on God's say-so, man was promised a subsequent reward. Man refused to be engaged in such a contract and the proposed faith-covenant was rejected by humanity's spokesman.

Salvation history records outstanding reenactments of the divine-human drama of faith. Noah, Moses, David, to name but a few from the Old Testament, were offered the gift by God; each responded with varying degrees of sincerity.

Abraham presents a good study of faith as proposed and accepted in the God-man communication. When God approached Abraham as the patriarch-to-be of that race which would be the vehicle for the coming of the Messiah, he was already a mature, worldly successful, personally content man. He was asked to relinquish these fruits of a lifetime to embark upon the new doings of a new career in a new place. Not an easy, not even an attractive proposition.

The enactment of this faith drama took place in an interchange of difficulties and rewards. Abraham was to leave country, family, and home to go to a strange land; but, though he and his wife were childless and well beyond their child-bearing years, his would become a famous name, for he would father a mighty nation. This nation would experience its existence in a state of bitter enslavement; yet Abraham's life-time yearning would be fulfilled in the birth of an heir; this already old man would enjoy an even longer life; and he would possess a land he could call his own.

When the promised son had grown into the fullness of youth, the young man was to be sacrificed as a holocaust in honor of the Almighty, even though this action would seem to be a negation of every promise that had been made to Abraham; but when Abraham's faith surmounted this un-dreamable obstacle, God intervened to forestall the sacrifice in order that through this son Abraham's descendants would be as "numerous as the stars, as the sand grains along the seashore." This great nation-to-be would overcome its en-slaving enemies, and through Abraham's posterity all peoples of the earth would be divinely blessed. ("And in thy seed shall all the nations of the earth be blessed...." How great the fulfillment of this promise in Jesus, the Messiah, who would come from Abraham's family to bring the blessing of salvation to all mankind in the new and eternal covenant of His Blood!)

Four points stand out clearly in this narration: God ap-proaches, a price is demanded, a reward is offered, man re-sponds with an open mind and a free choice. This quartet is the essential material of supernatural faith.

The pages of the Old Testament echo and re-echo the Abraham story of religious faith as it is cast in its four great facets.

The "I will be your God, you will be My people" refrain is God's invitation to faith in the prehistory, the formation, and final emergence of the Israelitic nation.

God's people were to pay the price of being different—of holding to their concept of the one, living God when the customs of all their neighbors pressured them to be like other men. Their personal and national outlook upon this world and the goods it offered was disciplined by a loyalty to God's will revealed in the law and the prophets. They conformed their temporal existence to a cultic worship which directed them in an eternal direction.

In return for their allegiance to God's directives, the descendants of Abraham enjoyed the protection of the Almighty in their times of loyalty and disloyalty alike. Under Yahweh's guiding hand they rose to periods of glory; through human blindness they fell into times of misery. Yet, in retrospect, the same providential care is clearly seen. God blessed His nation in its inner life and in its endurance in the march of history, giving to individuals and to the collectivity a richness in traditions and a heritage of messianic glory. They enjoyed a success in earthly measure against the array and magnitude of their enemies which was far beyond what their numbers and material resources would suggest.

Israel's response, again individually and as a people, to the approach of God formed a tapestry of many hues. Faith burned brightly, it faded into a paleness hardly discernible. It embraced the spectrum from robust in its intensity to feeble in its weakness; the "your God—My people" relationship to Yahweh at times commanded their whole dedication, only to be at other times almost totally forgotten in the traffic of worldly glory, material aggrandizement, and pagan idolatry.

The pages of the New Testament continued the narration of the great story of supernatural faith. The continuation and perfection of the "your God—My people" relationship was made physical in the God-made-flesh Person of Jesus and in His visible signs of healing, resurrecting, exorcising, of control over the elements and other material substances. These wondrous signs were based on faith and caused faith to take hold in those who witnessed them.

Of the many, many lessons on supernatural faith taught by Jesus in the course of His physical ministry on earth, an interesting example is seen in Simon Peter in the town of Capharnaum after the preceding day's miraculous multiplication of loaves. Jesus had completed His explanation of the bread fed to the multitude—that its real significance was to be seen in the contrast between the manna of perishable life before His coming and the Eucharist of imperishable life which His own Body would give.

In the light of the words He used, against the background of the Jewish law and idiom, contrasted with the natural abhorrence cannibalism generated in the minds of His hearers, Jesus, in this Eucharistic doctrine, was truly calling for a supreme act of supernatural faith in Himself, His power, and His word. He was appealing for that deepening of belief and trust which would transform the people from the imperfect "your God—My people" covenant signed in the animal blood of temple rituals into the fullness of that same covenant now universalized and perfected in the mystery of His own Person. In the words of the evangelist, the doctrine which He proposed as an object of religious faith was "a hard saying."

Indeed, to many of those who heard it that day, it was just that. Despite the many unexplainable—really unimaginable—wonders He had done in their sight (just yesterday the miraculous feeding; prior to that, physical and spiritual cures, raising of the dead, control of the elements), these followers doubted His power to deliver on His promise. Instead of previous experience eliciting an "How He can do this we do not know, but one possessing the powers we have already seen can do this also if He says He can," skepticism arising from a lack of faith turned them away from His discipleship—"I cannot understand, therefore I will not believe."

It was at this point that Jesus queried His chosen apostles as to their own faith in Him and the conclusion to which it drew them regarding a continuance of their association with Him. There is nothing in the sacred writing to indicate that the apostles were given or had a deeper natural insight into the proposed Eucharistic mystery than was had by the departing doubters. The difficulty of comprehension, the confusion of thought, was every bit as real in their minds as was the case with everyone else; the challenge to credulity was as much an assault upon their faith as upon that of each member of the crowd. In this moment of crisis, Simon Peter faced and resolved the dilemma of not understanding how it would be done but believing Jesus could do it. Simon Peter gave his response to the challenge: "Lord, to whom shall we go? You have the words of eternal life . . . and we have believed that You are the Christ." A sublime act of supernatural faith!

God had approached Simon Peter and elicited his act of faith by presenting to him a covenant-in-food which would be the guarantee of everlasting life. The price of submission through faith was to accept a doctrine he did not understand, to place himself outside of the mainstream of contemporary thought, to subject himself to the ridicule of the proponents of the stylish position, "...this is a hard saying . . . who can believe it?" But the reward for loyal belief was tremendous—apostleship unto the very foundation of the mystical Jesus, the Church!

The same "approach-price-reward-response" saga which is supernatural faith was retold on every page of the Gospel scripture. Therein God's approach to mankind was in the mystery of His own Incarnation and the life-giving message Jesus delivered to His contemporaries for an unceasing transmission to all men; it was in the auto-authoritative miracle-signs by which that Presence and those teachings were verified.

Man was called upon to open his mind so wide that he would sacrifice the natural conclusions of sense apprehension for the deeper insight which the eyes of faith gave, as when Simon Peter uttered his "You are . . . the Son of the living God," and was informed by Jesus that the disclosure of such knowledge was not the result of sense apprehension or even of merely natural faith; rather, it was the gift of supernatural faith given by the heavenly Father.

In supernatural faith, the will of man was asked to turn freely from immediate goods which conflicted with ultimate goals, even though these latter were known at the time only to the divine mind—for example, when Simon Peter and his companions left the fishing boats which were their livelihood to follow Jesus as their Master. The whole person of man was called to a trust in the Person and mission of Jesus, a self-abandonment to His way even if the pathway led to scorn and rejection, a commitment which, for that first band, led to death itself.

The reward was adequate—indeed, flowing over and above human expectation: "Everyone who has given up . . . for My sake, will receive many times as much, and will inherit eternal life." But, perhaps, as great in this life as in eternity, adherence to supernatural faith brought the reward of that revivifying privilege of witnessing to the messianic role of Jesus, to the verity of the "your God—My people" covenant by which alone mankind can fulfill the noble destiny for which the Incarnate God was sacrificed and in witness of which He arose to unending glory.

The response of man to God's approach is also recalled in the Gospel pages. The total response which built upon human persons the living edifice of the Church as it spread with incredible speed over the face of the earth; the partial response by which some passively followed the Christian way; the non-response by which individuals turned from the words of life to the death chamber of oblivion, and by which God's Chosen People refused the role for which He had nurtured them through difficulties and victories measured in the centuries of years of Israelitic history.

Supernatural faith, then, emerges from the pages of Sacred Scripture as a relational experience wherein God approaches man and man responds to the divine invitation. Supernatural faith always asks a price from man and carries a reward from God. It is the role of catechesis to inform man of the divine approach, that is, to open to the inquirer the full content of revelation; to elicit from man as total a response to God's invitation as the capability of the recipient allows; to show the excellence of the reward offered in proportion to the paucity of the price asked.

The exposition of religious doctrine finds no other source comparable to the Bible itself, wherein revelation and its history are set down under the direct influence of the Holy Spirit. This Scriptural presentation must always be in accordance with the norms of sacred tradition and the present teaching of the Church (to whom the interpreting role was divinely given), for it is the role of the catechist to build knowledge on facts, not on theories. The distinction between the Church as teacher and the theologian as investigator and theorist has already been made in these pages.

A similar distinction must be made between the theologian and the catechist. The former may investigate and propose new insights for debate and argumentation and new avenues of approach, for this is proper to his role; but the catechist is to instruct and form according to the mind of the Church, and this means the presentation of accepted and approved doctrine. While one person may be both theologian and catechist, the function to be performed under each title differs, and this difference ought always to guide authentic teaching. True, the catechist, to be effective, should read about and be familiar with new trends and thinking in the field of religion in general and Christian doctrine in particular. These varying theological theories of the day can be presented in the catechetical program—but always in such a way that they are clearly understood for just what they are: *theories*.

There are textbooks for the formal presentation of religious doctrine now available for the normal school grades (1 through 12) that do use the Bible as foundation and contain the authentic interpretations of the Church in the best of contemporary pedagogic methods. The task of the catechist is made much easier by the existence of such fine texts.

The catechetical task of eliciting a whole-hearted response to God's word is a challenging one. The mind of the recipient must be opened and attracted to the divine message. The goodness of God reflected in the superiority of the reward given over the price asked needs to motivate the will to a true act of love. The activated mind and will ought to arouse the emotions so that the entire person becomes religious, thereby adding through his apostolic spirit to every community of which he is a part the leaven which alone will renew all things in Jesus. The "Teacher's Manuals" which accompany the textbooks alluded to above are invaluable tools in developing a methodology to accomplish the catechist's difficult (but so rewarding!) assignment of securing the student's maximum commitment to religious living.

Supernatural faith is, as Vatican Council I defined it, the assent of the intellect to revealed truth, not because its own intrinsic truth is perceived by human reason, but because of the authority of God who reveals it. This definition, by referring only to human intellect, does not limit the concept of faith from involving the total person, as this has just been described. James, in his epistle, reminded his readers, "So faith also, if it have not works, is dead . . . by works a man is justified and not by faith only . . . for even as the body without the spirit is dead, so also faith without works is dead."

On the other hand, Paul admonished the Corinthians that if they had all gifts and bore all tribulations but lacked charity, it would all be as nothing. Yet charity rests upon faith. But even more pointedly, Jesus Himself set the norm: "Not everyone that says to Me, 'Lord, Lord,' shall enter into the kingdom of heaven, but he that does My heavenly Father's will." It is the clear teaching of Sacred Scripture that Christian life is not merely an intellectual assent, but a total person involvement, stemming from and activated by the stimulation and assent of the intellect to the specific, revealed truths.

Faith, then, can be viewed from three aspects: as the special grace which enlightens the intellect to accede to the truths communicated by God through His revelation—Jesus, the teaching Church, the Bible; the faith-motivated hope which is the movement of the human will to respond favorably to God's message because the content of that message is good and desirable as a pattern for human activity in this life as well as a goal to be reached in the eternal life; the faith-rooted love which motivates toward a Jesus-centered approach to life, springing from the goodness of God as Father and source of all blessings, and from the consequent love for self and neighbor as children, all in the same image of that divine Father.

Religious faith expresses itself in two general areas of human activity: to God in worship, to fellow man in charity and justice.

The entire concept of worship of God and the underlying rationale of the liturgy look to supernatural faith for their explanation. In the liturgy, by sacred signs, the individual as himself and collectively as the People of God acknowledges, embraces, and renews the "your God—My people" covenant. Through these rites God invites man to participate in the divine life which alone can raise him beyond the limitations of his humanity to the heights of an eternal, resurrected glory —imperfect in this life of earthly pilgrimage but fulfilled in the second coming of Jesus when this life is over.

Through these same rites man responds to the divine beneficence by renewing and elevating himself in the pursuit of his exalted destiny. Man's worship is most perfectly expressed through that faith which brings him to belief in the efficacy of those signs which acknowledge God as the source of all good and the treasury of mercy, as the supreme bene- factor who freely bestows his gifts upon his subjects. Thus the liturgical actions are the fullness of divine-human com- munication, for they unite God and man in one and the same action.

The expression of supernatural faith in the relationship of man to his fellow man is the outgrowth in action of a personal "I believe" to revealed doctrine. By a life pattern molded on the unifying principle of divine Fatherhood and human sonship, by an incorporation of self into the messianic role of Jesus, the Christian brings to fellow man and to human society the ultimate love-gift which is a knowledge of the saving truth, and the corresponding gifts of personal good will and service. In social justice, in equality, in the guarantee of human dignity, in alleviation of human suffering and need, in freedom and the fruits it produces, the true nature of the Christian message and the order it brings to human existence are made manifest for all to see. Through the man who lives as well as believes his Christian tenets God is made visible and known to other men.

Upon the catechist falls a good portion of the awesome task of moving religion from the realm of the idea to the world of action. Salvation history (as has been noted) is the record of God's involvement with real people in real life situations. This sacred record will continue to be written only in these same terms. And so the person in the marketplace of day-to-day living must be also the Christian engaged in the combat to snatch the man next to him from worldliness and renew him in the glory of the Lord. The Christian who is indistinguishable in his witness to the truths of Christianity from one who never heard those truths is a Christian upon whom the message of Christianity has been wasted. To learn is not enough—knowledge is a springboard to action.

The person imbued with the truth, the goodness, and the urgency of the "good news," particularly as found in the mes- sage of the Gospel, is the living witness to Jesus in the world of real people and their real life situations. Rooted in knowl- edge, witness is fructified in love—a genuine and intense love for Jesus as a here-and-now existing real Person; this love motivates Christian action from morning to night, every day of the week. The witness establishes personal relationship with Jesus alive and reachable in His Church, the Scripture, the liturgy, and in the person of his fellow man, especially, as Vatican Council II pointed out, those ignorant of God and bereft of human needs, rights, and dignity. Only the total complex of intellectual, volitional, and emotional love of a person for another person can motivate dedication of self to others. To live for Jesus requires just that kind of love!

The application and the spread of the Gospel message consciously becomes each one's personal responsibility. The physical Jesus sent apostles to speak His truth to all peoples, and they succeeded admirably because they were consumed with the greatness of the challenge. The mystical Jesus, the Church, must also send out apostolic witnesses equally convinced of the tremendous message they bear. It is the catechist in this day's times who is the arm of the Church to recruit and train the apostles for this great crusade of mission to the world.

Supernatural faith, then, is to learn from God's revelation: to come to a knowledge of God and in and through Him of life's goals and the way to attain them; to subscribe to these truths by an honest and total "I believe" commitment. Having done this much, then to exercise these beliefs oneself as well as to transmit them to others, both in content and implications. Thereby the contemporary increase in natural knowledge will be matched by an equivalent progress in religious belief, as the new information furnished by the former expands and modernizes the latter.

Thus renewed and revitalized by familiarity with the current doubts and obstacles raised by contemporary human progress and development, supernatural faith will most attractively display all of its facets—its looking into the future, its expression in terms of the present, its time-tested roots in the past. Fully developed and properly proposed catechesis will call modern man, even the skeptic, to abandonment of self-idolatry, to the life-giving word of God expressed and known through the ministry of Jesus.

To make this vocation apparent and effective to today's man, the old truths of religious faith are being re-armed with new weapons of catechetical methodology pertinent to present life situations. Through the dedication and zeal of catechists and those to whom they witness, inspired, enlightened, and strengthened by the Holy Spirit, this union of the old and the new of Catholic faith can conquer the world for God and renew mankind in the common brotherhood stemming from the one Father of all.

CHAPTER III

"In the Beginning . . ."

Supernatural faith, aided by the use of human reason, discovers in the Bible the basic principles of religion. The first three chapters of the opening book, Genesis, are rich in such source material.

The general atmosphere of the first part of Genesis is a reconstruction of events long since past. In this way, it is not an eyewitness account of the beginnings of the universe, of man, and the development of humanity upon the earth. All of these things had happened aeons before they were written about. As was mentioned in considering the origin of the present-day Bible, verbal accounts and speculations concerning the origins of things and the explanation of observed phenomena built up over the centuries. These stories constituted part of the literary environment from which aids were drawn by gifted men such as the Yahwist writer for the composition of their unique, spiritually oriented accounts. At a much later date these remarkable units of moral and dogmatic theologizing were edited into what are today the opening chapters of the book of Genesis. Different sources contributed to the biblical answer, "How did reality happen?" "Why are things the (immoral) way they are?" The first part of the book of Genesis (chapters 1—11) gives a written interpretation made in the light of revelation radiating from the Mosaic covenant and couched in an ideology with which people in the Fertile Crescent had been familiar for several millennia.

As was to be expected, the method taken to explain the inquiry "How did reality come about?" was equivalent to "How would I explain this thing?" The molders of the folklore of the Mesopotamian traditions, the inspired authors of the biblical narratives, the compilers and final editors of Genesis itself were limited in the answers they could give to the question by the intellectual and empirical horizons of their respective times, civilizations and religions. Thousands of years later, the progress of human resources would add, in areas theretofore not thought of, more extensive inquiry, deeper knowledge, and multiple factual conclusions.

This is as it should be; but it also demonstrates that twentieth-century approaches and emphases should not be demanded of those standing just beside the abyss of prehistory. To explain the origins and meaning of the reality which those pioneers beheld as the world, the people, and the patterns around them, the first people proceeded to use the material and norms proper to their niche in human progress. Hence the salvific truth of that time, guaranteed by divine inspiration, would come in forms of expression consonant with the cultural milieu.

As do we even in our age of advanced human knowledge, so too the gifted authors of earlier times wrote of sense-perceptible phenomena "as they appear to be." It is still the accepted manner of speech to consider the sun "rising and setting," to treat of reality in categories of gas, liquid, solid even though the basic concept of matter is that energy common to all atoms. Precise scientific writings would use more technical (and more true only from the scientific viewpoint) forms. But the understanding and expression of the common man remains modeled on the obvious character of things as grasped by his immediate observations.

The universe, as the non-scientist of the ancient Orient observed around him, was a flat earth covered by a domed ceiling finding its highpoint above the position of observation and tapering down to meet the earth's surface all around the circumference. In the dome were greater and lesser lights, some observable only in daylight, others only at night time. From this great dome waters periodically fell upon the earth.

The earth itself was part land and part water. On the land vegetation grew, animals roamed, insects crawled. In the waters various kinds of fishes swam; birds flew to and fro between earth and sky.

Under the earth was water, which, either of its own accord or through human ingenuity, came to the surface to blend with the waters falling from the dome or with those in the sea. There were also in or on the earth certain basic minerals which were adaptable to different uses and which could be altered in various ways to serve new purposes.

And upon this earth there was the observer himself and other creatures in great ways like unto him, yet in lesser ways different from him—for example, male and female human beings. This creature, man, was the master of the earth and its land and seas. Its night, day, and seasons, its minerals, vegetation, animals, fowl, and fish—all were man's to use and, so far as humanly possible, to rule.

The movement of the heavenly bodies, the interchange between night and day and the seasons, the intermittency of dry and rainy periods, all indicated to the observer an active force above the dome who regulated these movements and decided their purposes. This force was, indeed, a very important part of the reality which was being observed.

From all the parts and relationships man noticed in the world around him, he concluded that the universe was a constructed thing—the manufacture of an accomplished artisan, all of it conceived according to a plan and produced as an ordered working multiplicity of parts comprising one total existent. This high degree of order, regularity, and harmony was its own best proof that the final explanation of the universe could not be given in terms of chance or accident.

But even at that early point in history, a certain conflict within the total pattern of creation was already obvious. Man, possessor of the potential to nobility, frequently acted in quite an ignoble manner. In personal conduct and in relationships with other men, as individuals and as national collectivities, there were many instances of dishonesty, deceit, contention, plunder. The relation of man to the force above him was variable in its loyalty and in its appearances, so that many competing deities rather than one supreme ruler seemed the norm. Language, physical characteristics, material possessions, national rivalries differentiated and separated men despite the common nature they all shared. Man, seeker after pleasure, comfort, and immortality, was plagued with pain, suffering, and death. Good and evil seemed equally to share life's stage and to motivate man's actions. Even the ordered pattern of the inanimate was marked by occasional disorder, as when storms, floods, and volcanoes occurred.

Against this background of what was seen and what it seemed to imply, the authors of the book of Genesis searched for an expression of inner reality which would make these things meaningful to their readers. They had an advantage over non-Israelitic authors throughout the entire Orient: they could proceed to answer the questions with the unique insights provided by the revelations to the patriarchs and to Moses.

The challenge was answered in two separate compositions that we call the creation account (Gen. 1:1—2:4a) and the paradise account (Gen. 2:4b—3:24). The first account seems more methodical and detailed than the second, more in the human manner of building an edifice; the second tends to bring God very close, in the sense of God acting in human terms and by human faculties (anthropomorphism).

This first Genesis narrative on creation opens with the overriding concept of God as creator of all reality: "In the beginning God created heaven and earth." Notice that prior to this act there was God alone. He precedes all things, is superior to all things, is the ultimate cause and explanation of all things; before anything else was, God is.

The distinction between the creator and the created emphasizes the author's belief that his God is a different kind of being from those things which his contemporaries in other nations observed and knew—for the created is limited, God is limitless. Creation is an existence in time, God exists outside of time. The creative God is one, living, intelligent, powerful, the master of all creation.

In this manner the transcendence of God is underlined, even as the anthropomorphical presentation accents His immanence. These dual divine qualities need always to be borne in mind. Too intellectual a picture of God neglects His immanent activity in human life, while an overaccent on the immanence of God negates the role of His transcendence. God is at one and the same time infinitely independent of the human level yet personally and intimately involved in every creature's existence. True religious doctrine will always be conscious of this duality.

But the Genesis picture of God already presents the seed which later on Jesus will bring to flower in His revelation of God's Trinitarian life, namely, the Fatherhood of God.

As a father is one who gives life to his child in generating him, so does God give life to His creation and to each of us by bringing about and continuing a participation in His own existence. God truly is a Father. As a father transmits his own nature to the child he begets, so does God share His nature with men in the supernatural gift of grace by which the Trinity dwells in a human soul. God truly is a Father. As a father provides his child with the goods and necessities of life, with his own friendship and love, so does God in His providence supply man's needs with the good earth and human intellectual powers; He shares Himself with us " . . . not as servants but as friends," and measures His love by the infinity of His mercy. God truly is a Father. To God the Father, human creation's only fitting relationship is that of a loyal, loving, and grateful child.

The second verse of Genesis attempts to convey the nothingness which exists apart from the divine creative act by the terms "void," "empty," "darkness," "deep" and the formlessness of "water." Over this nothingness, however, God already was and was active. Using nothing but His divine will expressed in a spoken word, He would bring forth all the things about to be described in the calendar of a week of days.

While one reads these verses of Genesis, one cannot help thinking of the theological concept of true creation—the making of something out of nothing. This is the concept of creation in its pure meaning. Man says that he creates when he brings about an object which never before existed. But this use of "create" is an extension of the true meaning of the word, for actually man only "invents"—rearranges already existing things. The God of Genesis is not pictured as an inventor but as a true creator, hence possessor of total dominion over all things *in their very existence.*

The Genesis author, having introduced his subject, now enters the specifics of the divine activity. Picturing this procedure in the terms of human contractors, light was provided so that the worker could see the work he was doing; the materials of construction were separated one from the other— the light from the darkness, the sky with its waters above from the waters below, the land mass of the earth from the waters. Then the separate items of ornamentation were brought about: the vegetation with its reproductive seeds, the heavenly bodies of sun, moon, and stars, the sea creatures and winged fowl, the land animals and man.

In this very simple manner, Genesis explained the realities of day and night, of the changing seasons and the passing of time, of rain and water springs, of heaven and earth, of vegetable and animal fertility.

The origin of the entire universe and of all its parts was described as the work of an intelligent designer, working toward a known end, through the free choice of his will. Existing things were not, as pagan neighbors speculated, the product of some chance accident or of a war between competing gods. While such confusion of mind led other men to worship heavenly bodies or earthly creatures as gods, the God of Genesis was portrayed as infinitely superior to such things so that He was actually their source and reason-for-being. So powerful was the Genesis God that His word alone was sufficient to explain the existence of objects falsely worshipped as gods; they were powerless pawns, whereas the creating God was a provident being, that is, He ordered the laws of nature whereby things operated, and He determined the goals which they were to serve.

After creation God did not abandon or become indifferent to His handiwork; rather His activity continued it in existence and guided it along the pathway which He had determined and expressed in the laws proper to the varied items. The divine providence in Genesis provided life and the things necessary to sustain that life and make it full—light, heat, productive soil, animals for food and labor, and, in the human order, friendship of God and of fellowman.

By the creation account the misconception of two gods— the god of good, the god of evil—was destroyed. All reality observed in the created order was attributed to one God from whom these things came and by whom they remained in existence. Because God sustained them through a participation in His own existence, they in some way reflected Him, who is goodness itself. So it was that after each class of things was created God looked upon His handiwork and said of it: "It is good." Because all creation was good, it could come only from a good source. There was but one—a good creator —God.

The creation story spreads the divine activity over a period of six days; the seventh day is given to rest. This is a reflection of the Sabbath ordinance of the Mosaic decalog. There is to be a period of work and a period of rest after the work is completed. The Genesis day of rest, accordingly, is far more significant than merely a human custom; it teaches a human necessity. The span of six creative days so that a day of rest would be provided within the week was an intentional development of the Genesis author, for it conveyed deeper meaning. The progression of creation as Genesis presents it would have nicely allowed for man (to be the crown of the process, as we shall see) to have had a creative day (the seventh of the week) of his own; instead, the author placed human creation in the same period as the animal. Thus "God's day" of every week is given the same note of reality as had by the inanimate, vegetative, animal, and human realities of the universe. And thereby God typified the manner in which man was to say his "thank you" for the universe, for dominion over it, and for the marvelous gift of human life itself—one day of the week given back and devoted to God.

The Bible thus teaches in its opening verses that God has His day. Man can be busy about the things of his own world six days a week, but the remaining day he is to give up his pursuits in order to acknowledge God's preeminence in all human activity as well as man's thankfulness for and dependence upon the divine bounty. The day set aside from the things of man for the things of God directs human attention to the Supreme Benefactor, source of all blessings, goal of all creation. Thus man would express his own subjection to God's dominion; even here in time and on earth, on one day each week man would prefigure that eternal union with God for which he was made and toward which his life-activity should move him.

It is interesting to note at this point that the first two creative activities centered around light and water. From the introductory Genesis verses until the end of the total biblical book, these two elements play a central role in the communication between God and His people as recorded in salvation history.

Light is used as a sign of union with God, darkness symbolizes separation from Him. The divine pledge to the nation of the Chosen People was God's presence as a column of fire; the covenant of Moses and God was expressed in the light of Mount Sinai; the announcement that the Messianic expectation was fulfilled came through the light of the Bethlehem and the Magi stars; and St. Paul used the movement from darkness to light as a symbol of going from the despair of sin to the hope of justification. But the light-dark analogy reaches its highpoint in the Messiah when Jesus described Himself as "the light of the world."

Water played a role in many of the purification rites of the Old Testament, and its use, real and symbolic, recurs frequently throughout these books. Water was chosen as the vehicle for the destruction of the sinful world and the saving of faithful Noah; the Chosen People passed from slavery and into freedom by moving through the water of the Red (Reed) Sea. In the New Testament Jesus was revealed to the people at the bank of the Jordan, and the Trinity was manifested as He stood in the river's water. The bond of adoption into the family of God and the seed from which the life of virtue grows find their origin in the water of baptism. But again, the climax of the significant role of water as a symbol of God's favor is reached in the person of Jesus, who described Himself as the gift of "a fountain of water springing up unto life everlasting."

The absolute dominion of God over all the basic substances of the world, because the very existence of these things is entirely at the pleasure of the divine will, is verified and highlighted by Jesus in the New Testament. He walked upon water, controlled the winds, multiplied bread, changed water into wine, used common items in the performance of miracles. As Genesis identified God by His dominion over the elements of creation, so did Jesus establish His claim to divinity by exercising this same mastery.

Returning to the unfolding of the creation story in Genesis, the origin of the human species is treated more in detail than is that of the lower forms. The intention of God to create man in the divine image and to place him over the other creatures, and the actual production of man in male and female categories are recorded in the first chapter of Genesis. Man thus made and established in the order of creation is commanded to take up the task of multiplying his own kind, thereby populating the earth. On this note, the creation story comes to a close.

A second creation story, preferably called the paradise account, begins in chapter two, verse four. Herein the production of the universe is quite brief in comparison with the narrative already considered. In a few verses and in a generic form, the creation of the subhuman universe is unfolded. The creation of man is more detailed than it was in the first account, with separate descriptions and different occasions being given for the appearance on the scene of the male and the female of the species.

The biblical narrative teaches the unique nature of man which distinguished him in kind from all other animal creation: man alone was made in the image and likeness of God, that is, he dominated his environment rather than being dominated by it; he had the means to know "why" and the power to choose "how."

In addition to the dominion man enjoyed over all creation, he was to find in and through that same creation the pleasure and enjoyment which would make his temporal existence a happy experience. But that was not all. The good life was to be realized by male and female as mutual companions and helpmates, able to join together to share their lives and gifts with each other and with other human beings even as God shared Himself with them.

Genesis teaches the alikeness in nature and the complementary distinctiveness in role of the sexes—an equality in dignity but not an identity in function. Human sex, because it is a creation of God and thereby a reflection of His own goodness, is itself good and holy when its expression conforms to the divine idea upon which it is molded. Thus Genesis distinguishes the male contribution to the total creative pattern from that of the female, but always recognizing that only in both sexes are sex and human creation complete.

The function of sexuality is not limited to the reproductive act. In physical capabilities and psychological qualities man and woman differ. Yet life as it is lived by human beings requires the characteristic qualities of both sexes to fulfill it. The aggressiveness, daring, and strength of the male is complemented by the protectiveness, patience, and understanding of the female. As man and woman dovetail these and the other differentiating qualities of their sex, they bring about the teamwork by which the divine plan is accomplished, and thus reveal that sex in its fullness is not male or female but the cooperative blending of both.

The nature and purpose of sex is realized at the ultimate level in the fruitful companionship whereby new life is brought into existence. In cooperation with God, the male and female blend their individual lives into a common life which is at one and the same time neither of them and both of them. Through the revelation in Jesus whereby the inner life of God was made known in the Trinitarian mystery, sex would mirror in time the eternal, divine life itself—as the love of Father and Son personifies itself in the Person of the Holy Spirit, distinct in Personage yet identical in nature, so the human love of husband and wife produces in their child a new and distinct person, but yet the possessor of its parents' nature. The privilege and the responsibility of this august reproductive function controls and directs the tensions natural to concupiscence.

Genesis relates that humanity was created with natural perfections and a supernatural gift which were over and above the basic demands of human nature. In his human nature man was endowed with knowledge sufficient for his needs. Entirely above the capability of human nature, man enjoyed a love relationship with God—he was without sin.

So idyllic a situation brings us face to face with what is, perhaps, the greatest imponderable of reality itself and of religion in particular: with man so constituted in friendship with God, how account for the presence of sin and evil in the world of human behavior?

This problem of sin and evil has long occupied human attention, even as it intrigued the Genesis writer. Physical evils (such as storms, floods, etc.), are allowed in the providence of God for reasons which He alone need know, for God's is the absolute and total dominion over all that He created and ". . . it was good." The subhuman creations blindly follow this divine wish.

But the problem of moral evil, sin, is much more complex. The conflict between man's free will and God's signs of friendship constitute a formidable mystery, a problem man seeks to understand because it is vital to him.

The narration of the temptation episode in paradise provides an answer to the perplexing problem.

The excellence of man over all other creation is shown by the stewardship he exercises and the service the subhuman renders to the sustenance and enjoyment of human living. God's right of dominion over man is pictured in terms of the one tree apart from all the trees in the Garden—this one tree man was not to consider as his own or use as he willed. Adam and Eve understood and accepted the arrangement and abided by the divine prohibition, as is shown by Eve's reluctance to violate it, even to the extent that she argued against following the contrary course suggested by the tempter. God had set the rules for human existence, and humanity was following them—the blissful state of living portrayed by life in the beautiful garden.

But created in the image and likeness of God and free from sin and its tragic effects, man on earth carries within his nature a desire for infinity. Incapable of total satiation of his potentials, man ever seeks new sources for self-fulfillment. And in this area he would be susceptible to the suggestion that he, man, was not a mere image of God, but God

Himself; not a creature striving for infinity, but himself infinite. Evil struck at this vlunerable point, "...you shall be as gods."

The first temptation was placed in the human intellect and toyed with by the will. Instead of rejection because of its wrongness, man yields to the temptation's attractiveness, "...fair to the eyes and delightful to behold." Eve's choice was the apparent good of worldly delight over the real good of God's plan. Adam bowed to human considerations, choosing to follow the expediency of Eve rather than the wisdom of God. Thus a judgment based on human pride turned the created will from that of the Creator and put the former in rebellion against the latter. Evil was born of this inverted order of the God-man relationship, and the goodness which God had created into man was substantially negated. The coexistence of good and evil was explained—God created the good, man's rejection of God brought about the evil.

Genesis relates the sad effect of this human folly: sin, the loss of divine favor and death became the lot of mankind. In solidarity all men, from the first to the last, come under this state of sin—a condition known as original sin. Perhaps the theological argument is more clear and absolute when seen in reverse or from the Cross: because the saving work of Christ is absolutely universal, touching every human being who has existed or will exist, so too the sin that is expiated by Christ vitiates every human being from the first man in ages past to the last in some age to come. To deny original sin, then, is to deny the universality of Christ's redemption and to posit salvation apart from the Blood of Jesus. Could any blasphemy be greater?

As has been mentioned, in the events of the fall an opinion popular at the time of the Genesis story (and not even to this day quite abandoned), that the dichotomy in human behavior could be attributed to a god of good and a god of evil was refuted. True divinity was clearly shown to belong only to the Creator, and His work was good; evil was a perverse action of man's will to a free choice given him by God, a decision sponsored by an evil spirit. However, this evil spirit was not a God—this spirit could only suggest, not command; it was not a maker or ruler of things or persons.

Later revelation and Catholic faith identified the tempter as a fallen angel.

The fall also teaches that the making of moral law is God's prerogative. Man may desire other than what God decrees, and may even believe the "other" to be itself good. But "good" is not a matter of human opinions or majority consensus—Adam and Eve represented all humanity and formed a majority of two to one against God's directive. Yet the judgment of Adam and Eve that their choice was "good" did not change God's law, convert evil into good, or forestall the sanction imposed for disobedience to the divine authority. (A good counterpoise to the modern suggestion that morality depends on a "Gallup Poll" type of consensus.)

One final observation in the area of moral law and its objectivity reveals a single standard of morality for all human beings, and especially noticeable as being the same for man and woman. The ever popular conception that certain classes of humans can do things which other classes cannot, e.g., that it is permissible for a man to engage in certain immoralities while these same things are wrong for women—such discriminations find no basis in the Genesis explanation of the origin of evil. Humanity as represented by one man and one woman committed the same sin; each of them, man and woman, was judged guilty of the transgression; and each was punished and punished equally (if not identically) for violating the moral code.

Many pages of salvation history were to be written before this great drama of confrontation between the representatives of good and evil would be repeated—and then it would happen in reverse! When Jesus the Messiah came, He met the challenge of God's way versus man's way, and once again it was in the name of all humanity.

In its original representatives, Adam and Eve, mankind succumbed to the temptation of sensual desires and satisfactions by eating the forbidden fruit; to the temptation of flattery and vainglory by believing man could be God Himself; to the temptation to a materialistic existence by preferring the here-and-now created things over the future beatitude of the Uncreated God. The perverse choice made by Adam and

Eve plunged all mankind into the abyss of divine rejection—
no longer could it be said of humanity that ". . . it was good."

After His sojourn in the desert, Jesus, destined to act for
all humanity in the things pertaining to God, faced the same
evil spirit presenting the same deceits as bait to human pride.
Jesus, a hungry man, was offered the bodily desire and satisfaction of bread. He was invited to indulge in the vainglory
of showing off His own power by casting Himself from the
Temple spires. He was offered conquest of the material world
of people and nations in exchange for the spiritual allegiance
due to God alone. But Jesus rejected each suggestion for the
false goal which it is. In this act of turning His will to God
as end and purpose for being, Jesus reversed the choice made
by Adam and Eve. Jesus would continue this drama through
His public ministry until at its climax in resurrected glory He
would have lifted mankind back to the level of a supernatural
destiny—once again, at least potentially, it could be said of
mankind, ". . . it was good."

The Genesis story of creation is a saga of joyful beauty
and of ugly misery. But even in the drab verses of humanity's
eviction from God's favor with which the story closes, a very
bright ray of hope shines through for the future of the human
race. In condemning the evil of sin and the consequences it
caused, God also took issue with the tempter who led Adam
and Eve astray. God promised that the supernatural effects
of sin would be overcome by a future conqueror of temptation
and of sin: "I will put enmities between thee and the woman,
between thy seed and her seed: she shall crush thy head, and
thou shalt lie in wait for her heel." Jesus, the Messiah, seed
of the woman, would fulfill this promise in His victory over
evil and death.

The investigation of the first three chapters of the book
of Genesis indicates the rich storehouse of theological knowledge conveyed by means of a most interesting literary form
—a non-scientific, non-philosophical, everyday run-of-the-mill
human experience applied to the origin of the universe and
its phenomena. God spoke amply in the words of men trying
to explain the realities they observed around them through
the literary form of reconstructing the scene as these men
themselves would have undertaken the creative task.

CHAPTER IV

The Open Forum

The creation story presented in the opening chapters of the Bible suggests three inquiries of particular interest to modern catechetics—evolution, the first parents, and original sin. While distinct subjects, these three considerations are intimately connected one with the other. Which is not to say that all three are but one great cosmic upsweep and therefore all three must be treated always and only as one. They can, and sometimes should, be considered separately for they differ radically—subhuman, human, and dogmatic.

As has been noted, Genesis 1—2 actually embraces two distinct accounts, and these two records present their theology in noticeably differing forms. Further, logical difficulties present themselves as, for example, the creation of light before that of the light-giving heavenly bodies, man and woman created at the same time and at different times. Finally, the distinction between Scriptural content and container (the relationship between the divine message and the human literary form has been treated in preceding pages). In the light of these and similar factors, it is quite evident that the actual manner of the creative act is not dogmatically given in Genesis, nor was the Genesis author binding himself to a specific and accurate "how." Consequently, the Christian believer is not limited by faith to an acceptance of creation as the Bible verbally describes it. Evolution in its possibility and manner, therefore, is a legitimate area of inquiry.

Properly speaking, as was indicated in the earlier consideration of supernatural faith, faith should not be asked to exceed its essential capability by way of explanation or demonstration, nor should the methodology of this faith be directed to an end which is not its own. In the strict delineation of particular fields of human exploration, supernatural faith should not now seek from the creation account information which was not part of the original composition. Any concern of catechetics with the actual method of creation would be a secondary concern, one to be guided by the established findings of qualified scientists. To balance the record, the converse principle ought to be stated also, namely, that scientists should be primarily concerned with *how* the existence of multiple creatures ought to be explained from observable data; the scientist should leave to and learn from the qualified theologian's interpretation the ultimate source and meaning of creation.

The core theological point of the creation narrative is the existence of an all-powerful God who from nothing brought forth something. Whether the "something" was created all at once or in stages, whether it was one or more prime forms or a variety and complexity similar to the present pattern is not theologically deducible. For the advancement of human knowledge it is hoped that scientists in various branches of activity will find from the earth and its vegetable and animal population evidence leading to an answer to these alternatives. Much study and investigation has been, is, and will be given to these areas of wonderment, and to the extent that the findings of this scholarship rest on physical evidence, reason must accept them as true.

Insofar as scientific evidence leads only to a hypothesis, the credibility commanded by the postulates will represent natural faith. In the first instance, there can be no conflict with supernatural faith, for truth in one field must be truth in the other, as truth itself is one. In the case of conclusions resting on natural faith, if they differ from the theological fact they must be rejected. Supernatural faith is more credible than natural faith.

There seems no reason to contend that the Genesis accounts of creation (especially as detailed in the first account) and a development of the material world in great stages by an evolutionary process are incompatible. The succession of six days in biblical terms bears no judgment of any kind on the scientific concepts of great ages of material existence and emergence, and accordingly can involve no conflict with an idea of progression by stages of perfection to the "higher levels" which bear life and finally human beings. In such a vision divine wisdom expresses itself in ever greater manifestations of powers, and allows even deeper insights into the plan and purpose of all creation—up to life, up up to man, and up up up to God Himself! The fact of the matter is that either "all at once as is" creation or "primordial forms developing into greater perfection" are indifferent vis-à-vis God; the divine omnipotence is not enhanced nor lessened either way; consequently the theological (religious) teaching is the same.

The Christian approach to the question of subhuman evolution, as to its possibility and its methods, can be stated thus:

Evolution of created reality (except man) in a progressive way from one or many simple forms to the present variety and complexity of forms is admissible as an explanation of the universe as it now exists, provided that the role of God as cause of what first came into being and legislator/motivator of the laws by which it evolved to what it is, as to a predestined end, is acknowledged.

The evolution of man presents a more difficult problem, for man must be considered as a unified operating principle, the person, while still being understood as an entity comprised of a material body and an immaterial soul. The same rules for determining origin will not apply identically to man's body and his soul because each one differs radically in nature from the other.

Essentially there would be no theological difficulty in accepting evolution of the human body from some lower form.

As with the world below man in hierarchic order, the answer to "how" in the case of the production of man's body is within the proper sphere of empirical science rather than that of philosophy or theology. The only biblical text referring to the question is embedded in a context identical with that referring to plant and animal creation.

Although the subject of man's physical origins has intrigued scientific investigation for a long time, science has not been able to pass from the proposing of theories to the establishment of facts nor to a unanimity among scientists and their theories on the subject. Commenting on this in what is perhaps the most recent authoritative statement on the matter from the Church, Pius XII in *Mediator Dei* suggested caution in too quickly accepting bodily evolution for man insofar as the sciences have not yet presented any really universally accepted explanation of the scattered evidence pertaining to body structure. Above all, it must be remembered that the cultural advances of mankind since the last Ice Age are an entirely distinct area of research.

The soul of man by its nature precludes an evolutionary process as an explanation for its existence. Man becomes man by definition only when possessing an immaterial, immortal soul with an eternal destiny. The definition of man as a "rational animal" is entirely inadequate and erroneous.

The Bible explicitly describes this unique status of the human personality not in the Genesis accounts but in the body of Wisdom Literature, specifically the books of Wisdom, Machabees and Daniel. Since Protestant and Jewish bibles do not have these divinely inspired compositions, a most important key to the understanding of man and the Old Testament message is missing.

The information of the Old Testament was given more explicit precision in the teaching of Jesus regarding the immortality of the human soul, as, for example: "Do not be afraid of those who kill the body and then can do nothing further . . . fear him who has power to cast into hell after he has killed." "What does it profit a man if he gain the whole world but suffer the loss of his own soul?"

The immateriality of the human soul and its eternal destiny in heaven or hell points to the philosophical impossibility of evolving from a complex, material level of being to a simple, spiritual level. The soul described by such qualities is necessarily a simple substance, and this absence of parts allows nothing to rearrange from lower to higher form. Scripturally, theologically, and philosophically, supernatural faith affirms the non-evolutionary character of the human soul. (This position is not in any way jeopardized by the obvious movement of the soul as it "evolves" or changes from a state of ignorance to one of knowledge or from indecision to choice.)

The Christian approach to the question of human evolution can be stated thus: Evolution of the human body in a progressive way from lower forms falls into a category of research in which conclusions are based on available evidence. There is no special problem here because man is not man until endowed with an immaterial, immortal life-giving principle, the soul. We do not know at what stage in the process of bodily or physiological evolution this occurred. Evolution of man from the aspect of the human soul from lower forms to its present form is wholly inadmissible and impossible. Therefore, the origin of man as man, the unified operating principle —the person—(a thinking, willing, immortal creature in the image and likeness of God—a *different kind of thing* in nature from any other of the created), is by a direct and immediate creation of God. This in no way precludes drastic or fundamental changes in man's physical make-up: color, bone structure, size, weight, appearance from age to age or place to place.

While the foregoing presentation isolates man on an essential point from the categories of cosmic development which are the popular method of speaking about evolution, it is not thereby meaningless or outmoded. The physical characteristics of the universe and the sociological phenomena of humanity are understandable only in terms of man being ontologically different from both. Among all the things of creation man, by his nature, stands in a position of unique apartness. While sharing creaturehood with the other forms, man is distinguished from all the others (as if to form two general categories) by virtue of his deathlessness and destiny—attributes attributable to absolutely nothing in the subhuman world.

Between man as a person and the human behavior pattern there is also a real distinction, for the "person" is the source of the dichotomy of good and evil behavior. An individual man can behave nobly in one set of actions and ignobly in another; he can reverse himself and act ignobly in the very actions which he once did nobly. In view of this difference between man and the subhuman and the behaviorial, man in his origins should be considered separately from, and not merely as part of, the total created pattern.

The second inquiry of interest to modern catechetics concerns the origin of man as a distinctive order within the created pattern. Either humanity originated in the monogenism of a direct creation of one man and one woman, as traditional opinion holds, or in a polygenism whereby in an evolutionary process humanity emerged when diverse lines of anthropoids attained the human stage of development, so that the origin of the human race was a confluence of these many lines into one source. The increasing tendency of science to place the body of man into an evolutionary pattern leads some scientists to subscribe to a form of polygenism.

Those scientists who take a stand for polygenism seem to do so more because of the nature of their science and the scientific methodology proper to it than because of empirical evidence. Obviously it would be impossible to ascertain that a discovered fossil was that of a true human being as it emerged from animality to rationality and to state categorically that this exhibit was one of a given number or the only one of its kind. The first claim would be valuable only if all the fossils of that period and in that condition of transition were positively known, possessed, and studied. But who could claim to have all the fossils and to have missed none? Or, that the studies made from these ancient relics were so all-embracing and absolute in their findings and conclusions that theory was superseded by fact? The scientist, therefore, speaks in the group language of his profession—that if human life could appear in one bodily being, it could have and more likely did appear in a whole group of such beings.

If scientific proof of monogenism must rest on the demonstrable evidence that one and only one fossil represents the origin of the human race, then the scientist has no grounds (outside of faith) on which to state as a scientific fact a human origin from one specific person. And this for the very good reason that the singularity of *this* fossil must be indisputably established. How prove that another fossil might not eventually be discovered?

The basis of form change through an evolutionary process is closely identified with the "chances for survival" within the emerging form. Change produces casualties, so that the more hardy characteristics of the changing creature survive and the weaker ones perish. The best members of the emerging breed remain while the weaker ones disappear. Therefore, to secure a large enough number of survivors to make the changed form endure, there must be a relatively large base of origin. Hence to secure sufficient human beings to carry on the human race, there must have been a sufficiently great number of creatures emerging from animal to human so as, by natural selection, to weather the law of averages casualty list. Or so the scientific methodology says.

According to the scientific data, then, the evolutionary sweep is always up—the perfected survive and go on, the defective are destroyed and disappear from the scene of existence.

In the framework of scientific thinking the reverse process would be folly. To suggest that the vast numbers of human beings who have populated the earth resulted from the emergence of but two creatures—one male and one female—and that these two humans started the cycle on a higher level of perfection and then descended to a lower one would be "unscientific," hence repugnant to scientific methodology; to accept the proposal would require that reason be aided and uplifted by supernatural faith. But the "unscientific postulate" is precisely what traditional biblical religion has consistently proposed as the fact of the matter.

Those theologians who wish to win evolutionary scientists to the tenets of traditional religion, therefore, attempt to find means of expressing religious doctrines in acceptable scientific language and frames of reference. Thus the agitation on the part of some religious theorists to explain the origin of the human race in polygenistic terms rather than in Adam and Eve as two unique creatures directly created by God as human beings and the source of the whole human race.

The Genesis creation account should not be taken as a definitive teaching on the details of a monogenism vs. polygenism discussion. But in the *prima facie* meaning of the words used and in the imagery employed in the biblical description, the real individuality of Adam and Eve as the sole historically existing human beings in the Garden of Eden seems evident and has been accepted as such by the majority of the readers of the creation story for many centuries. (We really do not know how the original readers of Genesis understood it.) Subsequent Genesis writing as well as later Old Testament books witness to this common estimation. The New Testament also, and the literal meaning of the statements made by the teaching office of the Church corroborate the common estimation. There seems to be no positive evidence in these sources on which to base probability for a contrary theory.

Yet it must be granted that neither Scripture nor sacred tradition, nor even the living teaching office of the Church so precisely or explicitly treats the essence of the human origin or the exact formal objects of the statements in the Genesis accounts that the possibility of polygenism is totally excluded. If the polygenistic theory could be demonstrated by a proponent of it to be in true harmony with other related points of Christian doctrine, polygenism would no longer find contradiction in Scripture or Church teaching. The door is presently open—if only to the extent of the slightest crack—for such a theorist to step forth with sufficient proof of his thesis. And it must be admitted that it is through just such "little cracks" that theological speculation can carry on its necessary work.

It was in *Humani Generis* that Pius XII showed how difficult such a feat would be regarding polygenism when he wrote that the faithful ". . . cannot accept this view [polygenism] which holds that either after Adam there existed men on this earth who did not receive their origin by natural generation from him, the first parent of all; or that Adam signifies some kind of multitude of first parents; for it is by no means apparent how such an opinion can be reconciled with what the sources of revealed truth and the acts of the [teaching office] of the Church teach." The "crack in the door" is the word *apparent*—the polygenist bears the burden of making apparent how his theory can be reconciled with Scripture and Church—and some are trying as we shall presently see.

The theory of polygenism is not immune to serious questionings even from within the scientific community itself. The coincidence of diverse lines of anthropoids attaining to human status independent of one another, and then merging into that confluence from which would come one group essentially the same is a rather unscientific happening; science is not likely to find co-dwelling with so problematic a chance too much to its comfort. Further, science recognizes the need to admit that (unless it were pure chance and thus totally unscientific) if such a process occurred once it could occur again. But not a shred of evidence indicates even a remote second time. Why? Finally, science can present no positive evidence in refutation to monogenism, even while arguing, because of scientific methodology, to its opposite.

Perhaps it might be fitting at this point to recall that Christian faith—if we are absolutely certain that the tenet in question is truly a tenet of faith—is above the natural level. If to make such a tenet of supernatural faith palatable to naturalists its supernatural aspect must be abandoned or seriously diluted, then what has been gained? The scientist has not been converted to the religious understanding but rather religion has died in its capitulation to purely natural faith based on reason alone. If the scientist, and rightly so, expects the theologian to accept science in its own frames of reference in those things properly the object of science, then should not the theologian expect others to accept theology according to the particular methods proper to it? To deprive religious truth of the element of miraculous divine intervention can neither credit religion nor lift naturalists to the supernatural.

There is no essential incompatibility or insurmountable barrier between science and Christianity, as the great numbers of Christian scientists amply demonstrate. Why, then, try to formulate a fictitious fence?

The third subject of renewed theological investigation deals with original sin. Because the Catholic position on evolution of the human body and on selection of the monogenism postulate over a polygenistic one seems related to the doctrine of original sin, this doctrine is being reviewed for possible points of compatibility with evolution and polygenism.

The traditional position of Christian doctrine is to view original sin as a free, historical act which turned one human will from the will of God. Because this one person (Adam) was the principal of the whole human race, he acted in the name of the entire human family: one person, one act of rebellion (disobedience), one result—solidarity in the effects of sin proper to all mankind.

The current desire of some Christian theologians and exegetes to find a common term of expression for the scientific and religious communities has led to a renewed investigation within religious teaching of the precise doctrinal limits of original sin. The unicity of man and the universality of human sinfulness must be the accepted starting point of the investigation, for these things are of defined faith.

Perhaps the crux of the whole matter concerning original sin is its vital connection to the entire body of Christian beliefs, as these are held to exist in Sacred Scripture and Tradition, in the teaching of the Church and in the universal opinion of the faithful.

Pope Paul VI reminded the participants to "A Symposium on Original Sin" in July, 1966, of this centrality: ". . . the mystery of original sin has very close connections with the mystery of the Incarnate Word, the Savior of the human race, with His passion, death, and glorious resurrection, and hence with the message of salvation that has been entrusted to the Catholic Church." The eye of the needle through which any new view of original sin must squeeze is that area which does not seem to be totally closed to interpretation, namely, the precise nature of the message in the original, formal judgments of given verses of the Bible. None of the relevant texts have as yet been officially interpreted by the Catholic Church.

Bearing in mind that the rethinking of original sin is not specifically for its own sake but rather better to accommodate to the theory of polygenism, it will be of value to reconsider the traditional position of Christian doctrine regarding original sin.

The strongest Scriptural statement concerning original sin and its effects is stated in the Pauline epistle to the Romans:

"... as through one man sin entered into the world and through sin death, so also death passed into all men because all have sinned.... By the disobedience of the one man, the many were constituted sinners."

The Council of Trent rested heavily upon this apostolic teaching and in this mind *Humani Generis,* previously quoted, concludes that the doctrinal difficulty against a polygenistic origin of man is due to "... original sin, which proceeds from a sin truly committed by one Adam, and which is transmitted to all by generation, and exists in each one as his own." The weakest part of this statement is "transmitted to all by generation," a phrase found nowhere in the Bible or in early patristic writings.

The Second Vatican Council, while not treating of the dogma of original sin as a specific item, nevertheless referred to it in the traditional usage of the Church: "Although he was made by God in a state of holiness, from the very beginning of history man abused his liberty, at the urging of the Evil One. Man set himself against God and sought to attain his goal apart from God."

Pope Paul, in addressing the theologians and exegetes at their original sin symposium, expressed his conviction that "... original sin, with regard to its existence and universality, and also its nature as a true sin . . . is a truth revealed by God in various passages of the Old and New Testaments." Note that neither Vatican II nor Pope Paul alludes to "transmission by generation" as vital to the original sin dogma.

The proposals being offered as an alternative for the traditionally held doctrine of original sin vary with the thinkers and authors who treat of the subject. Yet certain common strains are discernible in all the theories. In summary, the common denominator of sinfulness found in all men is explained in the newer proposals by attributing it not to human beings but to life-situations shared by mankind, in environmental influences, in the perverse atmosphere about us—all summed up as "sin of the world." Thus sin as known and experienced in individual lives is not so much a state of alienation from God due to a precise action of the will as it is an attitude of man toward God's offer of sonship. A supposed upward, preordained evolutionary pattern of man was thwarted or redirected by the fact of sinfulness, so that "original sin" was not the loss of an already possessed state of grace but rather the failure to achieve the perfected state which was the "to be" goal of evolution.

Against this sort of theorizing stands the faith of generations of Christians, namely, that sin in a particular life and sinfulness in men in general is an effect of a first, personal sin which deprived man of gifts over and above human nature's due with which God had endowed man at his creation; the original sin of Adam is the root cause of all men being deprived of God's grace and favor and love—of becoming a *massa damnata* (to use St. Augustine's words) until the advent of the Savior, Jesus.

The traditional teaching on original sin is more easily grasped and understood because of its natural simplicity than are the more complex (and often tedious in detail) alternative proposals offered by the "evolutionist" theologians and exegetes, even allowing for their sometimes clever insights and ingenious circumlocutions. Also, the common teaching bears the endorsement of Scripture's literal sense, the Church's normal teaching, and the universal consensus of religious faith. Until such time (if time can accomplish it) as the very formidable difficulties of the "new" theories on original sin are overcome and the Church officially endorses those theories as valid alternatives to the present teaching, good catechetics cannot include them as "facts" in its presentation of Christian doctrine. See further, the observations already made on page 48.

To close the "Open Forum," it might be well to add a word of caution against "fad" approaches to catechetics. Good catechesis will always be on the alert for better methods of presenting Christian doctrine and encourage new insights into it. To do otherwise would be to stifle progress, kill off the ever developing organism of a living religious message, and blunt the opportunity to direct lives to Christian living. But across the stage of the last few years have passed approaches now hardly mentioned—question and answer, kerygmatic, biblical, anthropological, historical. All had their good points, and the ideal catechetical method would be a perfect balance of all within one methodology.

It has been likewise with the names of individuals—literally "fan clubs" for theologians, exegetes, and religioscientists (and their pseudo images), and too often the "fans" showed less concern for the solidity of doctrine than for the image of their hero's popularity. Many of these names are now forgotten and others are approaching that fate.

The only "cult" compatible with Christian catechetics is that which is formed upon Jesus as He expresses Himself through the Bible, sacred Tradition, and the teaching Church. When individual catechists polarize around some other figure, as if he were the Messiah and as if the Church knew not knowledge until his advent, it is quite probably explained by the (St. Paul's phrase, "itching ears") novelty of a "new doctrine" or a "popular fad." It should be suspect; fads pass quickly, leaving their erstwhile champions looking quite silly, while divine truth traditionally held and taught endures and its adherents bask in reflected wisdom. It is better to utilize a proven broad base for understanding rather than to go to the narrow extreme of one particular contemporary approach or person, for genuine renewal is not pursuit of the novel but a refinding or refurbishing of the eternally true essentials. If subsequent study proves the new is authentic and not merely a fad, then is time enough to embrace it as solid doctrine.

To distinguish the new of true renewal from the falsity of fad catechetics (or theology), it is necessary to follow Catholic newspapers and periodicals which report what the Pope and his Commissions say, for these voices propound true doctrine. If catechetics for today and tomorrow is an expression of Vatican Council II (and it must be!), it must teach what the august Council taught as it is interpreted and promulgated by the teaching Church. This message will be the call to renewal and the specifications of what renewal embraces. Renewal is to move into the present time and situation the truth and goodness of the past, not to create an entirely new and novel content of faith. To do the latter is not renewal but revisionism. Authentic Christian doctrine will always be "apostolic" in the creedal sense of the word.

CHAPTER V

In the Interim—Part One

God's Genesis promise of one who would conquer evil and restore to mankind the supernatural destiny for which it had been created was to wait a long time before its fulfillment in Jesus, the Messiah. The events which prepared for and led up to this most unique and wonderful of all happenings would be many and varied. The pages of salvation history would record great and mysterious interventions of God as He worked out His divine plan, and just as many remarkable and perplexing responses to that plan on the part of man.

The Genesis writer set the stage for these future events as he continued the narration of primordial history.

Chapter four of Genesis opens with an account of Adam and Eve as parents of flesh and blood offspring, their sons Cain and Abel. One was a shepherd, the other a farmer. Rather than living in a state of fraternal charity, they are pictured as in contention one with the other, and as standing, one in a position of divine favor, the other in divine rejection. The short narration comes to a climax in the first recorded fratricide.

It is quite likely that the Genesis writer in this chapter is writing beyond the limits of a brother-to-brother event. In the farmer role assigned to Cain and Abel's role as shepherd can be seen a picturization of the tension within the human race in its underdeveloped stages—the stable farmer opposed to the nomadic shepherd as the farmer strives to protect his lands from the roving exploitation of the latter. Translated into today's terms, we could cite the contention between the rural population and the city dweller as each strives to secure greater benefits from the Government at the expense of the other, or the discordance caused in the economic and social pattern of a nation as industrialization and agriculture compete as a way of life.

In the mentality of the original human authors of Genesis, Abel might well be a representation of the Chosen People in their early history, for they were a roaming people, keepers of flocks of sheep. Therefore Abel is cast as the virtuous favored of God and the innocent victim of premeditated evil on the part of Cain. Those who chose the material gods of the created world and who were attached to these idols as a farmer is to his fields were represented as wreaking this evil upon God's people. As a sign of this rejection of God as Lord, these people would perpetrate any crime—even murder of God's elect. In the Cain and Abel episode is seen a reflection of the Adam and Eve choice of the material world in preference to the spiritual life God ordained for them.

Another possible insight into the Cain-Abel event lies in the opening verses of the fourth chapter. These verses could be a preamble to the historical struggle of that nation chosen by God as His own against nations honoring polytheistic false gods. Abel is the pre-sign of Israel while Cain represents the nations of pre-Christian Gentiles.

In a broader view, Abel may represent righteousness and allegiance to Yahweh, the true God, among the Chosen People, while Cain represents those of the elect who were disloyal to the "your God—My people" covenant and chose in its stead a way of idolatry as a life pattern.

Still another interpretation can be drawn from Cain and Abel by identifying them with the events of the preceding three chapters of Genesis. In this view, credence may be given to this fourth chapter narration as a third source of the creation story. Herein Abel is the good creation coming from the hand of God, while Cain represents the evil introduced into creation by a mankind too attached to the goods of the earthly, material world. Especially in verses eleven and twelve the original happy estate of mankind can be seen as taken away as a penalty for sin—for the refusal of the human will to pattern itself upon the divine plan.

Any of these symbolic meanings of the Cain and Abel event can be interpreted as substantiation that this scene represents broad divisions of humanity rather than two specific individual humans. The generalized view is strengthened by the quickness with which the narrator enters into a broad-based genealogy in the last ten verses of the chapter—an indication that the human race had gone far beyond the bounds of two sons of the original parents.

Of more interest for the field of catechetics is the divine message contained within the narration of chapter four.

Of first significance in theological meaning is the clear teaching that the original sin of Adam and Eve had been transmitted to their offspring. As the primal father and mother of the whole human race, their sin thereby became the common trait of sinfulness found in every member of their posterity —in all of humanity. (By divine intervention, the sole exception is Mary, the mother of the Messiah, Jesus.) This sinfulness and its consequence as a common human inheritance are verified by St. Paul (as was noted in the previous chapter, *In The Forum*), and Jesus attributed His mission on earth to the need for overcoming the effects of sin. Cain and Abel thus represent the experience of each human being, namely, that sin multiplies sin.

Sin as a human act—judgment by the intellect and choice by the will—is indicated in this fourth Genesis chapter, as is the fact that sin resides in the will-act and not in the judgment; sin is shown as the choice to move in the direction of known evil, not in the intellectual suggestion to do so. This latter is merely temptation.

The duality of temptation and sin has already been mentioned in considering Eve's approach to the forbidden tree; it is seen again here, as God cautions Cain of the lurking occasion of sin (temptation) and the means whereby he "...shall have dominion over it." Even though human nature has been tinged with sinfulness, it is still within man's power to overcome temptations to sin and, indeed, his bounden duty to do so.

Cain and Abel teach mankind that once man refuses his loyalty to God as the Father deserving the fullness of human love, it follows that man will reject his fellowman as brother. All the sins of man against man, all the social injustices of class against class, and all the strife between nations is succinctly explained in Cain's cryptic reply to God, "Am I my brother's keeper?"

In the narrative of the relationship between these two brothers the message of the seventh day of creation is reaffirmed. Despite man's rejection of God by sin, the original obligation to offer worship still endures. Because Cain and Abel offered in the same kind as the gifts they had received from Him (animal, farm produce), this act of worship is to be one of recognition of God's goodness, His total dominion, and man's limited stewardship over God's gifts.

In this powerful drama of Cain and Abel, God's providence is shown as extending to all men, and even those who reject God, if they repent, are still the recipients of His protective mercy. Cain's sin had to be punished and it was, by the divine edict that the earth should resist his tilling and he should be a roaming fugitive. But God tempered His justice with mercy and kindness, and He gave Cain a special mark of protection so that no one would do him harm or unduly persecute him.

Despite God's benevolence and patience, the Genesis writer saw sin ever accelerating and enveloping more people more totally. The increase of sin increased the wrath of God. Finally the divine judgment against human wickedness reached its climax in the story of the Flood.

Two distinct accounts of the Flood are presented (as had been the case with the creation episode), with points of difference occurring in various details. The accounts are not presented successively as was creation, but are interspersed one with the other.

In essence, the narration records this story: Wickedness had so multiplied itself among mankind that ". . . all the thought of their heart was bent upon evil at all times." God repented that He had created man, and resolved to destroy all life upon the earth. However, one man, Noah, and his family were found to be righteous and therefore deserving of the protection of divine providence. Noah was instructed to build a ship which would carry him and his family, and sufficient and varied livestock and fowl to sustain life after the destruction had taken place. When all of these preparations were completed, God sent water upon the earth in such great quantities that the whole earth was covered with water, thereby destroying all life upon the earth save Noah and the occupants of his ark. When this destruction of life was accomplished, the waters receded and the ark dwellers returned to the land. God commanded them to multiply and renew life upon the earth, and He promised that never again would such a deluge be sent to obliterate evil.

The historicity of the Flood has received at least a degree of verification from the recording of a similar disaster in non-biblical literature of ancient times and from the findings of archeological and geological research. But the extent of the water's coverage of the surface of the earth and the extent of the destruction caused by the flooding are not quite so evident. There is nothing in the Scriptural rendering of the Flood story or the beliefs of the teaching Church which would preclude seeing in the terms of universality and totality used to describe the Flood anything more than the use of an author's technique of emphasis. To make his point, what happened in a limited area and to part of the living creation was emphasized by magnifying it to maximum proportions.

The theological content of the Flood narrative is based on the depths to which sin and its consequences extend. Sin separates man from God, his source and supply of life and purpose; this loss of divine favor dooms man to an irreversible death, in which all of his eternal potential is destroyed. Thus the state of sinfulness to which the human race had progressed caused God to disassociate Himself from His creature man and to symbolize this severance by the sign of death—to man and to all the subhuman creation over which he ruled and upon which he depended for life and its needs.

In this narration, the justice of God is made manifest. Man's rejection of the "your God—My people" covenant, brought about by sin, was a truly free act of man. Man, by his nature an image of God, is a responsible being. Therefore, God, who promised rewards for man's fidelity, as a just God must punish man for his infidelity. Thus the faithful Noah and family were spared from punishment and given the means to continue their lives; the unfaithful others were meted out due punishment for their sins by being deprived of life. In this episode is prefigured the day of final judgment at the end of time which Jesus described to His followers.

The Flood story also reflects the inherency of divine worship. Noah, upon emerging from the ark, built an altar and offered holocausts of the animals and fowl he had saved. Thus he acknowledged the majesty of God and gave thanks for the divine protection afforded him.

Many centuries later, Jesus would take the substance water which had destroyed mankind because of sin and use it in baptism to destroy sin in order that mankind might be saved. Just as Noah had won favor with God as signified by being saved from destruction by riding upon the waters, so would mankind ride into justification by the water of this sacrament. Finally, the ark which weathered the ravages of the Flood to carry Noah safely to the shores of a new life prefigured the Church of Jesus which would carry the faithful through the troubles of temporal abode into the glory of the new life in Him.

Man thus purged, re-created in a new relationship with God, and commissioned again to the multiplication of the human race carried ahead the saga of the God-man covenant which is salvation history. The Genesis writer expresses the forward march by giving a genealogy of the children of Noah and the nations they founded. The author thus explains the expansion and diversification of the human race among many nations.

In this parable, the unicity of the race is pictured as a common language of all men, and of all humanity as a group of travellers going from a former place (pre-flood?) to a new location. In this new place (post-flood?), the populace decided to make provision against another catastrophe such as they had just experienced. They would build a tower so high as to be safe from future destruction by flood and would thereby be able, by their own making, to have access to their God in His heavenly kingdom.

The quite advanced state from the Flood days of this thought is reflected by the historically latter custom of building "high places" for the worship of the pagan deities. As the Israelitic nation lived among its pagan neighbor states in later centuries, these "high places" of the infidels were a constant source of temptation to polytheism for the monotheistic Hebrews. So it is quite possible that the writer of the Genesis account, looking back upon the Flood episode, borrowed this imagery from his contemporary neighbors. Thus the more primitive forefathers were cast in the pagan role—they, too, would build a tower at the top of which would be their Yahweh.

The evil of the tower concept was twofold: it showed a distrust in God's promise that no future flood would be visited as a divine punishment upon the human race, and it reflected an idea and a hope that man could save himself by his own means and efforts and independently of God's assistance.

To refute these two false assumptions, the Genesis author writes of God's displeasure at this human effort and expresses the divine wrath in terms of confusion in language and the dispersion of the proponents of the tower plan to the areas of various countries of the world.

The Tower of Babel imagery was brought to the fullness of reality much later in salvation history, and again, as has been noted of previous types, in reverse of the original presentation. The people of God depicted by the Genesis writer in the Babel episode were dispersed and differentiated by a confusion of tongues; the new elect, the People of God of the eternal testament, were unified and given a common heritage on Pentecost Sunday when, because of a gift of the Holy Spirit, man's multilingual separation was overcome by all men hearing the apostolic message in one universal language.

The great tragedy of Genesis in these opening chapters can be summed up in this observation: the expulsion of Adam and Eve from Paradise, the contention between Cain and Abel, the destruction of humanity in the waters of the Flood, and the rebuke of human design at the Tower of Babel show the total wickedness of sin and the absolute meaninglessness of man in rebellion against God.

The lesson to be learned from these sad events and their even sadder consequences is that the man who would maintain his proper relationship to God—a loving child to his good Father—will not do it by separation but by union, and the most exalted external form of union for the Christian is in an interior, meaningful liturgy. Observance of the Lord's day, celebration of the Mass, encounter with Jesus in the sacraments will renew the highlights of salvation history in individual lives and make more viable the earthly People of God. The use of intellect and will and of created goods in the worship of God will reverse the order of sin whereby these same things were used to rebel against God. Thus will each successive generation of mankind re-enact, perpetuate, and hand on the experiences of their forebears and restore all things in Jesus so that God's words at creation will echo throughout time: "it was good."

CHAPTER VI

In the Interim—Part Two

Having portrayed the origin, development, and meaning of the primordial world, the Genesis writer turned his attention to the beginnings of his own people as a nation, the Chosen People of God.

This section of salvation history (as did the previous part, but now more specifically) looks forward to the central point and figure of the salvific action, Jesus. Indeed, without Him as its fulfillment, the history of a "Chosen People" would seem to be an exercise in futility. The Old Testament expectation is of *something, someone.* Without fulfillment of this expectation, the question might well be asked: "Why a chosen people at all?" or, "A people chosen for what?"

Thus, in the persons and events which the Old Testament authors record in the successive books of this section of the Bible, the Christian must see the planting of the seed of salvation and its development in the time and place situations of the Israelitic nation. Christian doctrine does not study the Old Testament for itself alone, but as a means of developing the perspective and focus which will finally reveal the Messiah Himself—Lord and King of all history.

The seed already planted in the original state of human creation and the messianic promise that the offspring of the woman would crush the power of evil begins to grow and take on form in the history of Abraham's posterity.

In the chapter *The Faith*, God's call to Abram to assume his place in the drama of salvation has already been considered. In return for his act of faith, God re-established with him and his progeny the "your God—My people" relationship, and in name and in fact designated him as *Abraham*, "father of My people."

An interesting sidelight is inserted into the Abraham story by the mention of Melchisedech, his offering of bread and wine, and the blessing. Melchisedech springs into the story without identification from an ancestral line and fulfills the dual role of king and priest: king of the future divine city and priest of the Most High even before establishment of an official priesthood. He offers to God's People (in the person of their progenitor) the food of bread and wine, and accepts from them the ritualistic acknowledgment of divine supremacy, the tithe. Then he blesses Abraham in the name and power of the most high creator, God. In the New Testament, Melchisedech and these events are seen as paralleling Jesus Himself (Jesus so used the episode) and the new priesthood which Jesus ordained to carry on His eternal testament. To Abraham, at the very beginning, was given this prefigure of the future messianic event, for which the Abraham vocation was to be so important a first step.

In the course of time, the divine promise to Abraham was fulfilled and the son Isaac was born to him and Sarah. Isaac married Rebecca and became the father of the twins Esau and Jacob. The latter received the blessing and heritage of his father and became the vehicle for perpetuating the divine promise of a great nation. By several wives Jacob fathered twelve sons who, in turn, generated the twelve tribes of Israel. (God decreed that the name *Jacob* should be replaced by that of Israel. This name then represented both the individual person and the whole nation.) The sons of Jacob were Reuben,

Simeon, Levi, Juda, Issachar, Zabulon, Gad, Aser, Dan, Neph-thali, Benjamin, and Joseph.

Joseph was sold into Egyptian slavery by his brothers where, by his power to interpret dreams, he rose to a position of rank and trust. During the great famine (which he had foretold), Joseph was in charge of rationing the grain. His father Israel sent his ten sons (keeping Benjamin at home) to Joseph for food. Joseph knew who they were, although they did not recognize him. He prevailed upon his brothers to bring Benjamin to Egypt, and when this had been done, Joseph made himself known to his brethren and besought them to bring their father also to Egypt. Thus Israel and all his clan, with all their possessions, encouraged by a vision from God, departed for a new existence in the land of Egypt.

Joseph is seen as a prefigure of the fulfillment of God's promise which was to come at the highpoint of salvation history: Jesus was rejected by His own people and His closest companions, the Apostles, even as Joseph had been by his brothers. Jesus was bartered into the hands of His persecutors, just as Joseph had been sold into the hands of the antagonistic Egyptians. Jesus forgave the offenses committed against Him and brought the means to a new life; Joseph absolved his brothers for their previous crime against him, and provided them with the necessities for preserving life. Joseph the bene-factor was a figure of Jesus the Savior.

Israel and his sons settled into the life of Egypt, and with the passing of years the Patriarch was gathered back into the bosom of his forebears; his son Joseph followed him. The favor which this immigrant family enjoyed with the ruling Egyptians lessened and finally disappeared as new rulers arose.

In the days of the Israelites' suppression by the Egyptians, a child was born to a set of parents of the Levi tribe. He was reared in an Egyptian household by a daughter of the Pharaoh, who gave him the name Moses. Upon reaching manhood, Moses visited among his own people and saw the hard life imposed upon them. To avoid possible persecution for the killing of one of the oppressors, Moses fled from Egypt. He married, reared a family, and enjoyed a settled existence in the employ of his father-in-law.

God, in the form of a burning bush and upon holy ground, appeared to Moses and commissioned him to deliver the descendants of Israel from Egypt for the purpose of forming from them a chosen people. God ordered Moses to do this difficult task in the name and by the power of "Yahweh, the God of your fathers, the God of Abraham, the God of Isaac, and the God of Jacob...." And Moses, with his brother Aaron, went down to Egypt in obedience to God's command.

The Pharaoh, however, was most adamant in his refusal to allow the slave people to go from Egypt. The Exodus (second book of the Bible) author relates the contention between Moses and Aaron on the one hand and the Pharaoh on the other.

Moses and Aaron, at God's command, brought a series of disasters upon the land and its inhabitants in order to pressure the Pharaoh to release God's people. Each sign was effective in accomplishing its purpose and moved the Pharaoh to give in to Moses' wishes; but each time the affliction was lifted, the Pharaoh reneged on his promise.

These marvelous signs are depicted in Exodus as ten great plagues, each one of which affected the lives and goods of the Egyptian people. The first nine plagues were: river water changed into blood, an overrunning of frogs, an onslaught of mosquitoes, an epidemic of flies, a plague of boils on man and beast, a destructive hail storm, a scourge of locusts, three days of total darkness.

Scriptural exegetes have seen in the narration of the plagues a blending of various sources of tradition into one written account with an adding of local color to the basic happening. Some authors see natural phenomena of the area pictured as supernatural events in the Scriptural rendition. Others believe that events and reflections of later times were written into the original story. Be these theories as they may, the rapidity of one event following upon another and the dramatic manner of presentation clearly reflect the author's intention to express a miraculous divine intervention.

In preparation for the sending of the tenth and final plague, God directed Moses and Aaron in the manner of preparing a commemorative meal. Meat (lamb or goat) roasted, unleavened bread and bitter herbs comprised the menu, and the quantity was not to exceed the needs of one meal. The doorposts of the Israelite houses were to be sprinkled with the blood of the meal's animal.

At this point in Exodus, the author also describes another ritual, that of the unleavened bread. It is a fairly common thesis that both of these celebrations preceded the historical scene in which Exodus places them—one as a ritual of animal raisers, the other of an agrarian community. In time, both celebrations merged into one common event historically associated with the tenth Egyptian plague.

Yahweh decreed that the ritual meal and the unleavened bread become a sign of His deliverance of the Israelites out of the captivity of Egypt and that it should be celebrated annually, with an explanation of its significance, down through the ages. Because it commemorated the exemption from death of the Israelite first-born when the angel spared the houses marked on the doorposts with the animal blood, and due to its association with the exodus from Egyptian soil and domination, this ritual was named "Passover." God further decreed that henceforth the first-born of Israel's children and livestock should be dedicated to the Lord as a commemoration of the power and favor by which He spared them at the time of the liberation.

The tenth, and decisive, plague was the death of all Egyptian first-born, human and animal, from the house of the Pharaoh to that of his lowliest Egyptian subject. When this tragedy struck, the Israelites, with all their families and possessions, were given leave to depart from Egypt. Because the Passover Meal had been eaten and all was in readiness, the great exodus got underway immediately, the Lord leading His people as a cloud by day and a pillar of fire by night.

But once again the heart of the Pharaoh was hardened, and he, with his army, set out in pursuit of the Israelites. At the Red (Reed) Sea the confrontation between the followers of Moses and of the Pharaoh was about to take place when the Lord miraculously opened the sea for the safe crossing of the Israelites and then closed its waters upon the Egyptians as they tried to follow.

The miracle of the waters at the Red Sea is attributed by Exodus to a strong wind, a gesture of the hand by Moses, or to the relocation of the guiding angel and the cloud from the front to the rear of the column of Israelites. Whether one or all might have been the instrument which effected the saving of the Israelites and the destruction of the Egyptians (or whatever variant interpretations modern exegetes may put upon the event), the Exodus author is clearly indicating divine intervention causing miraculous results.

Once safely across the water and free of their pursuers, the Israelites began the trek to the holy land of Yahweh. It was to be a long, hard, and many times disappointing journey. But God would be with His people in cloud and fire, and for the sustenance of the travelers bread (manna) and quail would fall from the heavens as Yahweh's gifts.

The passover from the bondage land of Egypt to the road to the promised land "flowing with milk and honey" is the highpoint of the entire book of the Old Testament and perhaps the most direct link between the Old Testament and its prefigures which the New Testament fulfills.

The slavery of the Israelites under the tyranny of the Pharaoh was a sign of the universal human bondage of men chained by the wiles and machinations of the "Tempter to Evil" first met by mankind in the Garden of Eden. The greatness promised to Abraham, that his posterity would be a mighty nation, was carried in the hearts of his heirs as they awaited the coming of the leader who would convert promise to reality—a hope God fulfilled by sending Moses to them; mankind after the Fall still carried in its heart a yearning for the infinite, and waited, even if unconsciously, for the leader who would fulfill the Genesis promise of a heel to crush human imprisonment by evil—and Jesus came as that liberating leader.

The Israelites were saved by the blood of the passover lamb from the death God decreed as a punishment for the wickedness of evil ways, as the salvation of all mankind from eternal death would be made possible by the blood of the redeeming Jesus. The followers of Moses were led into their new life, and the forces of evil which sought to snatch this opportunity from them were destroyed by passage through the water of the sea, even as the followers of Jesus, born into a new life, would break the dominion of Satan in the waters of baptism.

The memory of God's providential care of the Israelites was kept ever fresh by the re-enactment of the passover meal; the new nation of God would continue the mystery of its deliverance in the celebration of the Eucharist, in which the manna of old became the bread of everlasting life. The eyes of the original pilgrims were set upon their promised land, while the pilgrims to the parousia look forward to the heavenly kingdom. The Israelite saw in the exodus of his ancestors the singular sign of God's guiding intervention for that nation; the Christian recognizes the salvation mystery accomplished in Jesus as the most unique sign of God's universal love. Moses was the shadowy sign of God's promise; Jesus is the clear sign of God's fulfillment. The exodus of the Old Testament points the finger of God directly to the mission of Christ.

Within the third month after the deliverance from Egypt, the migrant Israelites had reached Mount Sinai. The people camped around the base of the hill, while Moses went up to its higher regions. Here he conversed with God and was promised that the Israelites were God's very own people; three days later, in confirmation of His offer, God appeared in the form of fire, thunder, and loud trumpet blasts. Moses went up to the top of the mountain and received the law of the covenant, the Ten Commandments. The "your God—My people" relationship was formalized.

The new People of God were to receive their charter, too, in a scene reminiscent of Mount Sinai. The Apostles, gathered in the upper room on Pentecost, received God's spirit in the form of tongues of fire, amidst the manifestation of the natural phenomenon of great winds blowing, and the apostolic voice was heard as a mighty trumpet of the new covenant.

A sidelight to the whole Mosaic story and to the making of the Sinai covenant is the awe inspired by God's presence and the sense of holiness which surrounded the place where that presence was made manifest. At the first meeting of God and Moses, God made clear the awesome approach of man to the divine presence, "...for the place whereon thou standest is holy ground." At the climactic, pattern-setting encounter on Sinai it was not different, and Moses was to instruct the people, "Take heed you go not up into the mount, and that ye touch not the borders thereof." The God of the new covenant is the same God as of old, and while He is approached now in love and intimacy, He should not generate less awe—especially to the point of vulgar familiarity. Truly Jesus is our brother—but He is also our God!

After the great articles of the covenant had been delivered to Moses, the Exodus author concludes his work by setting down a record of other laws—of justice, for judges, relating to the sacred things, the tabernacle, the ark of the covenant, the altar, the priestly vestments.

The third book of the Bible, Leviticus, details the reasons, materials, and means of various cultic worship acts and ritualistic procedures governing worthiness and unworthiness, cleanliness and uncleanliness, various religious feastdays, and related subjects. Leviticus is particularly concerned with the place of eminence afforded to the tribe of Levi, for its members were of the priestly caste.

The next biblical book, Numbers, gives a census of the tribes of Israel. This book also prescribes religious ceremonies and the laws governing them, especially as these matters affect the Levitic priesthood. Numbers continues to narrate the rebellious spirit of the people against the providence of God, and expresses God's punishment upon the people, namely, that no one who was delivered from Egypt should live to enter the promised land, not even Moses himself.

The last book of the Pentateuch (five books—the *Torah*, the law), Deuteronomy, recalls former history, reiterates the previously given laws and adds some new ones. The general mode of this book is three discourses by Moses in which he reminisces about the experiences of the Exodus and its subsequent events. The people are reminded of their infidelities and God's mercies, of His providential care; they are exhorted to remain faithful to the covenant, continue the tithe and firstborn offerings, and observe the God-ordained religious festivals. Moses promises that Yahweh will raise up a new prophet from the nation for all the brethren. This prophecy has traditionally been interpreted as a promise of the Messiah. The "your God—My people" covenant is reiterated and the rewards for fidelity as well as the punishments for violation are recalled.

Finally, this last of the great five books of the Old Testament Bible closes with Yahweh taking Moses to a mountaintop where he is allowed to see the Promised Land. After this, Moses dies and is secretly buried by the Lord. Josue, the son of Nun, became the leader of God's people by command of the Lord. Deuteronomy closes with this great tribute: "And there arose no more a prophet in Israel like unto Moses, whom the Lord knew face to face—in all the signs and wonders which He sent by him, to do in the land of Egypt to Pharaoh, and to all his servants, and to his whole land."

* * * * *

The one word which underlies and summarizes the first five books of the Bible is *covenant*. In its biblical sense, covenant differs from the secular meaning of contract; the latter indicates a negotiated agreement between equals in which there is a giving, a getting, and a period of endurance. When covenant is used to depict the "your God—My people" testament, a relation of unequals is described. God is so superior to man in the order of existence that only total benevolence on His part can explain a divine-human partnership. God offers undeserved gifts, man returns required faithfulness. The idea of covenant runs throughout salvation history and is the catalyst giving continuity to the pattern.

It must be clear that God is under no necessity whatever to enter into a covenant relationship with the creature man. God owes nothing to man, cannot be given anything by man, essentially speaking; on the other hand, man is totally indebted to God, receives everything from God, and lives to return to God. It is because of divine love and goodness that God calls man to partnership with Himself, asking only that man respond in love and fidelity.

In Adam and Eve the first divine-human covenant was proferred. Divine love and goodness created mankind in these two persons, gave them a nature dominant over all creation, made them in Its own image and likeness. God bestowed upon the first man and woman gifts of natural perfection and supernatural capability, and asked in return only a loving fidelity to His holy will. The covenant was accepted and bliss prevailed. But as time passed, Adam and Eve proved unfaithful to the divine benevolence and the covenant was remitted.

Notice that this covenant between God and His creature was a direct arrangement and embraced the entire human family—God and Adam forged it together, mankind acting through the first parents as through its principle.

As a beginning point in the long journey to re-establishing full friendship between God and man, Noah, a just man, was chosen by God. As a sign of his good faith, Noah was asked to sever his earthly ties and to trust in the divine providence; his reward would be the role of "second father" of mankind. Noah proved faithful to his commitment to God's will.

Next, God chose a family and called Abraham and Sarah to relinquish physical comfort and security in order to sow the seed of a future people. In return, his abandoned hope of fatherhood would turn into an offspring who would father a mighty nation and the hope of the world. Abraham and Sarah responded to the divine invitation and lived faithful to it.

Finally, God chose a people. Moses led the children of Israel out of their bondage, forged them into a nation, and delivered them to the land which would be their own national home. Moses and his followers were asked to relinquish material security for the opportunity of being spiritually free men through whom God could execute His great design. Despite grumblings and occasional lapses, the Nation of God took its place among the peoples of men.

Notice the progression: what all of humanity had lost was being restored by a selective process among humans—individual, to family, to nation. Notice also the approach: God directly made the first offer to humanity, but the subsequent offers He made through delegates—Noah, Abraham, Moses. The creation of the renewed eternal life followed the creative pattern of the original—God directly created and then used man as steward of the bounty; the original creation was represented as fully developed, but replacement would be by natural growth from lesser to greater, from seed to full flower, from child to adult.

Also, it should be noted that God's covenants, promised at their making to be of long endurance yet terminated prematurely, do not make God's promise undependable. The long endurance was predicated on man's fidelity; when this reciprocity was not forthcoming, God justly withdrew His offer.

The covenant pattern was not yet completed; to go full circle, once again it would need to be offered to all mankind in a direct action by God Himself. The new Adam would give an affirmative response to God's goodness toward man and thereby reverse the ill effect of the first Adam's rejection of the covenant.

The new and eternal covenant came to all mankind in the perfect humanity of Jesus; it came directly from God in the true divinity of Jesus. The covenant was expressed in a God-man Messiah—decreed in the will of Jesus' divinity and accepted in the blood of His humanity. In this unique Person the Old Testament as promise of a restored Eden was fulfilled and the Testament of the new Eden was begun. That is why Jesus stands at the crossroads of human and religious history, truly its central figure.

A study of the Old Testament covenants shows a development of a religious consciousness among God's chosen people as they lived out the historical events of people existing among other people in a common world of many facets. It would be a grave mistake to consider the covenant people as already fully aware of their role in God's salvific plan or as dwellers in a purely idealistic, spiritual environment. As a more specific law, distinctive doctrines and forms of worship developed, God's people gained a deeper insight into their part in salvation history. Israel became an organized, recognizable society of men in the world, yet specifically identified with the one and living God. However, the full implication of this growth can be seen only in retrospect, only after Jesus fulfilled the law, perfected the doctrine, sanctified the worship with His own blood. Then the organized, recognizable society of men in the world, the Church of God's People, identified the one and living God for the whole world as long as that world exists.

Every time a man turns his mind to God, engages in prayer, performs some religious ritual, he is incorporating himself in the historical covenant relationship with God. This worship of God by man is under the guidance of divinely proclaimed beliefs and laws; it is within the framework of religious pattern according to the society of man among which one lives.

But true religious worship is not confined to these formal areas alone. The "your God—My people" covenant permeates every daily-life activity—work, study, recreation. The covenant must be as constant on the part of man as it is on God's part. God continually provides His benevolence, especially in the continuing creation by which one's very life is continued in existence; every human act should be an act of gratitude and glory for such generosity. Catechetics finds teaching and practice in the liturgy, and the liturgy should be the showplace of catechetics, the liturgy as performed in church and carried out into life's contacts and activities. In that way God and man meet and walk together on the pathway to true and final human fulfillment as the names of the "little people" take their place alongside those of the "big heroes" on the roll of salvation history.

CHAPTER VII

In the Interim—Part Three

The balance of the books of the Old Testament Bible narrate the story of the Israelitic nation's place in its historical period of world events. These books give an account of a particular people living in a world community of other peoples. Israel was a distinctive group because it was chosen by God for a supra-worldly purpose; yet it was also like unto its neighbors, for it was a political entity existing in a specific time and place. So the history of this people in its aspirations and its failures, its successes and reverses, its harmonious contribution to world order and progress, as also in its wars and competitions in the secular society does not differ materially from that of the neighboring states.

But through all of the worldly happenings Israel was still the unique society—it was God's Chosen People and its activities truly contributed to and formed the record of salvation history. Secular and religious aspects in the other nations were distinguishable, but in Israel they were one and the same, namely, the covenant offered by God, the response to it by man. To the Israelite of Old Testament times, the phrase "separation of Church and state" would have been meaningless.

Yet it must always be borne in mind that Israel's pre-election by God did not make these people different in their humanity from other people. To understand and to accept the story recorded in the books of the Old Testament it is necessary to be mindful that these were real people, with human strengths and weaknesses, ambitions, competitions. Thus the narration contains some sensual and materialistic aspects. To reject the validity of the biblical people as God's chosen nation or to repudiate the biblical books as being true salvation history because of the secular and carnal aspects is to miss the whole point of the story. The record of God's people and of salvation history is the story of real people—and the Old Testament Bible gives a vivid picture of real people. But in the depths of worldliness, these were a people whose purpose (even when it was being ignored) was that of witness to the reality of Yahweh to the neighboring nations.

This one and singular dedication might well hold out a model for the Christian world of God's Chosen People. In Israel all things were the working of Yahweh and the response to His benevolence on the part of His people. That which was good—fertility of field and womb, military success, long life, and much more were signs of man's fidelity and God's rewarding favor; the opposite of these goods was the sign of God's displeasure caused by man's unfaithfulness to the covenant. Every aspect of human life, no matter how commonplace or stupendous, was a sign of the "your God—My people" relationship working itself out in human events. The role of the Israelitic nation was a Yahweh-centered one in the most basic sense of the idea.

The activity of Israel in the history of humanity was to be a link—looking back to the merciful promise made to mankind in Eden and forward to the presence among men of the Messiah who would fulfill that promise.

Point by point consideration of the remaining books of the Old Testament is more properly a study for specialized Scripture commentaries than for this present writing. Many excellent commentaries and explanatory studies are available for those who wish to pursue the investigation. For an orientation to the new Christian catechetics a brief survey and a mention of outstanding persons encountered in these biblical books, insofar as these reflect highpoints of salvation history, will suffice.

With the death of Moses and the ascendancy to leadership of Josue, the Chosen People entered and took possession of their promised land. The Christian sees in this leader and event a prefigure of what was to come: Josue (in Hebrew the same name as Jesus) fulfilled the prophetic promise of Moses and led his people into the land "flowing with milk and honey"; Jesus, fulfillment of all the prophets, leads all mankind into the promised land of eternal bliss.

The remaining historical/legal books of the Old Testament record the division of the new homeland among the twelve tribes of Israel. A loose confederate form of fraternal interest united the people under a series of "Judges."

In this biblical usage, Judges are not merely officers of a court of justice as they are in modern terminology; the Judges of the biblical account are men who were actually governors of the territory and its inhabitants. The nation under the Judges was, as mentioned, less a nation than a confederation of somewhat autonomous tribes; the principal message conveyed by the books of this period concerns the unfaithfulness of the people to the covenant, the punishments visited upon them for their infidelity, and the returns of the people to compliance with the covenant terms.

The last of the line of Judges was Samuel, who, bowing to the necessities of the times and the wishes of many of the people, anointed Saul as a kingly type of ruler. Because all the tribes accepted Saul's rulership to a degree no one man had had in the time of the Judges, he became the first in the line of Hebrew kings. A powerful, single human ruler met resistance from those who believed such an arrangement was an affront to the sovereign and unique position of Yahweh as Head of His People. The forces who wished to conform the nation to the pattern of the surrounding states, which were ruled by kings, prevailed. Israel became a monarchy.

Saul was succeeded as king by David, who eventually was able to hold (at least nominally) the allegiance of those tribes in the northern as well as those in the southern part of the land. Under King David's effective military leadership, not only were the bonds of union between the twelve tribes strengthened, but the land was defended against the aggressions of neighboring states and expanded in territory and influence.

David chose Jerusalem for his capital and had the Ark of the Covenant brought there as its proper home, intending to build a fitting temple of Yahweh for it. Most important for Christian catechesis is the messianic role David and his kingship were to play in salvation history. As foretold to David by Nathan the prophet, from that royal house would come the future king who would also be Lord. Also, King David has been pictured by history as Yahweh's chorister to whose composition were attributed many of the liturgical hymns which formed a backdrop for the Messiah's appearance.

Solomon, son of David, succeeded his father as monarch. Solomon worked to increase the centralization of government but by the end of his reign had succeeded only in driving the northern and southern tribes into separate nations. Perhaps the most significant aspect of Solomon's kingship was the great temple of Yahweh which he built in Jerusalem and which became the focal point in the worship of Yahweh, the enduring symbol of the Chosen People's unity as a nation set apart, and an always to be revered memory in the pages of the New Testament gospel.

After Solomon, the northern tribes formed the nation of Israel with its capital at Samaria. A long series of kings occupied its throne until, in 721 B.C., the nation was destroyed by the Assyrian army.

The southern tribes of Judah and Benjamin formed the nation of Judah with Jerusalem as its capital city. The kings of Judah were all descendants of the line of King David and endured until 587 B.C., when Judah was conquered by the Babylonians.

In this double collapse and conquest Yahweh displayed His wrath at the infidelity of His people. Their continual flirtation with pagan gods and cults, their consequent ignoring of the "your God—My people" covenant moved God to destroy them as a nation and to level their city of Jerusalem and its temple. The survivors of the catastrophe were led into captivity in Babylon and the tragic period of exile began its half century of duration. Yet, as had happened so long ago at the

Flood, a small number of the heirs of the patriarchs remained faithful to Yahweh; and upon this remnant God would eventually reconstruct and carry on His plan of divine benevolence and friendship.

After the return from the Exile, the biblical books represent the prehistory and patriarchal periods in genealogy form, then a second version of the glory of the original monarchy, particularly the glories of David and Solomon. These accounts retell the great advantage of fidelity to Yahweh and the covenant.

The reconstruction of the elect nation is symbolized by the restoration of Jerusalem as the holy and capital city, especially as seen in the rebuilding of the temple and the city walls. Though under foreign political domination, the Chosen People enjoyed sufficient autonomy so as to be identified by profession of the Yahweh faith and the religious principles upon which it rested. In this liberty God manifested His faithfulness to the covenant.

The historical/legal books of the Old Testament end with the record of the Jewish military and political resistance to the forces (internal and external) opposed or indifferent to the nation's law and temple traditions and characteristics. Herein is revealed the tension between allegiance to the traditional Hebraic ideals and the later-day effort to conform to Greek and Roman concepts. The destiny of the nation was reiterated —the Chosen People exist that God might draw from them the fulfillment of the great promise.

These latter books also reveal the development, deepening, and sharpening of detail within the Israelitic theology, particularly the monotheistic viewpoint, man's immortality, resurrection, reward and punishment after death, intercessory prayer for the dead.

The wisdom literature of the Old Testament accents the individual living of the good life—as a naturally good thing in the earlier books and more specifically as a religious commitment in the later books. In teaching a preference for virtue and the avoidance of vice, the providence, justice, and mercy of God, and God as the source and purpose of wisdom, man's reason-for-living was directed to a higher than merely natural plane.

The final great division of the Old Testament is the prophetical books. However, prophecy must not be considered as confined solely to these books; Moses and Nathan are but two examples of great prophets situated in other than the books of prophecy.

The prophets were singular men in the hierarchy of persons in Israel. Prophets were men called by Yahweh to be His representatives in fulfilling a specific task: to inform the people of God's will. These inspired men spoke, not on their own authority or wisdom, but by God's command and to enunciate His directives.

The prophetic message of the Old Testament cannot be held exclusively as a "foretelling of the future" in the sense prophecy has in contemporary language. The ancient proclaimers of God's word spoke to the people of their own day about situations of their own time; the abuses they mention, the reforms they demand, the punishments they threaten, the rewards they promise are to be understood by the people as having current application in reference to the "your God—My people" covenant. Particularly did the prophets stress the Mosaic tradition and its ethical monotheism.

In the fuller light of subsequent history, these same messages will be understood as also having had a content for the future, so that they are seen as God's means for furthering divine revelation—this role becomes clearer as the prophecies are realized in the reality of the Messiah.

It would be far beyond the intent of this book to study each of the Old Testament prophets and the message he brought to the unfolding drama of salvation history. Rather, these many messages can be sketched in the broad outline of the picture they give of the Messiah to come. He would spring from the seed of Abraham, the tribe of Judah, the line of David; son of a virgin mother, the Promised One would be born in Bethlehem at the time of the second temple.

The Messiah would be the Son of God, the Prince of Peace, humble, meek, and merciful, worker of great signs. He would be the prophet, priest, and king of a new kingdom. He would propagate true knowledge of God, suffer a cruel death, arise from the dead, and be glorified by Yahweh.

In a career of striking contrast, the Messiah was portrayed by the prophecies as a suffering servant and a triumphant king.

The fulfillment of the promise made to the principals of the human race in the Garden of Eden, pledged to Abraham through his posterity, reiterated to Moses and the Hebrew leaders down through the centuries was to come in a real flesh and blood living person dwelling in the midst of God's Chosen People. The divine message was like a great mosaic—the pieces were gradually arranged by successive prophecies and the national and individual mentality prepared by centuries of human history. Thus it is unrealistic for us to expect that the Jewish nation should have perceived the prophecies concerning the Messiah with the same precision that the Christians, with the benefit of hindsight, were able to have. For the Hebrew, revelation was a step-by-step development, over a very long period of time, of a messianic consciousness; to Christians, Jesus is a real, living Person dwelling in their midst.

The saga developed within the covers of the Old Testament is not antique and discarded; it is not meaningless and forgotten. The Old Testament forms the solid foundation upon which the New is built, and as such is revered and kept alive in the covenant of the New Testament people. Nowhere is this more true than in the most sublime act of the New Temple's exalted liturgy, the Eucharistic Action.

In microcosm, the first few minutes of the Mass bring before the participant's mind the whole sweep of pre-Christian salvation history: in the sign of the Cross, the preeminence of God is acknowledged in a salute to the eternal Deity. Man's fall from the original state of human innocence and his subsequent sinfulness are recalled in the recollection of personal sins and the plea for forgiveness. The centuries of messianic yearning find expression in the readings from the Old Testament books, while the fulfillment of their promise and the climax of salvation history are proclaimed by the reading of the good news of the Gospel. The role of the prophets of old is perpetuated by the homily, in which the enduring prophet of the new dispensation, the Church, performs its role of teaching God's People. The gathering together of the congregation into a community of God's children is symbolized by the worshippers presenting their petitions to the Father in heaven in the Prayer of the Faithful. The affirmative response of God's People as a pledge of covenant fidelity is given in the recitation of the Creed.

While the time and events of the Old Testament era are recalled and renewed in every celebration of the Mass, the Church also emphasizes these fundamental happenings in its liturgical year by celebrating the Advent season—the time "coming up to" the birth of the Promised One. The liturgical texts of this period reflect the anticipation, the urgency, the holy impatience of God's People for the promised Messiah. Each year thus renews, with its joys and blessings, the birth of the Savior which happened physically so long ago. The incarnational renewal of people and things is perpetuated in the projection of the Incarnation to the limits of place and time. Thanks to the living liturgy, the renewed present joins as one with the expectant past as both look with hope to that future in which all will be glorified in the image of the resurrected Lord. Jesus, the Messiah, first-born and model of all creation, Prophet, Priest, and King, is, indeed, *the* reality of all time, and the living liturgy continues His work in its every action.

* * * * *

When the fullness of time was willed by Yahweh and the Genesis promise was about to be realized, the incarnational renewal was at hand. Then the last and the greatest of the prophets emerged from his desert retreat preaching repentance for sin and a return to covenant fidelity. As had his prophet-predecessors of old, John the Baptist made known the will of Yahweh, proclaimed the divine wisdom, trumpeted the word of God. But now it was not as seeds which would flower in some future age; as had been foretold, the precursor announced God's will, wisdom, and word in their immediacy and fullness, in flesh and blood. From the bank of the Jordan, with finger pointed to a physical presence, rang out the long-awaited good news: "Behold the Lamb of God! Behold Him who takes away the sins of the world!"

The Passover of the new Exodus—the Messiah present in flesh; salvation proclaimed—salvation history at its crest; Jesus revealed—God dwelling among His people!

CHAPTER VIII

"Your God---"

"Ye men of Israel, hear these words: Jesus of Nazareth, a man approved of God among you by miracles and wonders and signs . . . . you by the hands of wicked men have crucified and slain . . . . God hath raised up . . . . hath made both Lord and Christ, this same Jesus."

In these words did Peter, the chief of the Apostles, proclaim to the world the good news which inaugurated the messianic age. The expectation of the nations was fulfilled and the Christian message of salvation was introduced—words to echo through the centuries until time would no longer be measured.

Peter—Simon of the fishing fleet—made his momentous proclamation from the basis of his personal association with Jesus of Nazareth and through the supernatural enlightenment of faith given to him by the Spirit of God. In companionship with eleven other selected associates and from the accumulated experience of innumerable witnesses to the public career of Jesus, Peter extracted the essential meaning of Jesus' ministry, namely, that the promise made long ago by God to the progenitors of humanity was accomplished in the existence of this one Person. The interim covenants which kept in being the "your God—My people" relationship were finalized in an eternal arrangement. The Old Testament had closed, the New opened.

The story of the events leading up to Peter's profession of faith is recorded in the four biblical books of the Gospel.

Under the inspiration of the Holy Spirit, and drawing upon the resources of the Christian community and witnesses of the contemporary scene, the authors of Matthew, Mark, Luke, and John establish through the life-events of Jesus that He, indeed, was the fulfillment of the prophecies sprinkled by God throughout the history of Abraham's posterity in the pages of the Old Testament.

In the Gospel account are provided guidelines to the ancestral origin of Jesus in the family of King David, birth in Bethlehem of a virgin maiden, and announcement of His arrival by the precursor, John the Baptist. Jesus is portrayed in the Gospel as a meek and humble man, yet also, almost paradoxically, as the recipient of the public clamor that He be made king. The humiliation of His suffering and death and the exaltation of His resurrection and ascension form the climax of the Gospel biography.

The evangelists thereby identify Jesus as the fulfillment of the prophecies made of old to the Chosen People and treasured by them through the centuries in their sacred books, temple worship, and national purpose. In the aggregate, Jesus stood pre-eminently as the anticipated suffering servant and triumphant king—judged king by Herod, the chief priest, and the scribes at the time of His birth and proposed for royalty by cheering crowds during His life; seen as a humbled and obedient servant in the cruelty of His persecution and execution which, it was thought, terminated His life at Calvary.

The historical preparation for the Messiah was not limited to prophecy, however; it was also expressed in the concepts of law. Thus the writers of the Gospel give witness to Jesus as the summit in this aspect of Jewish life.

The law was given to Moses and through him, as a covenant, to the people of his nation. Through the centuries of their existence the law was promulgated, refined, and expanded as the national and messianic needs required. The Gospel portrays Jesus in terms of this law, not as merely a further extension of the established pattern, but as its finalization: "I have come . . . to fulfill it." In many instances, but especially in the *Sermon on the Mount*, the new era is delineated in phraseology contrasting the old order of Mosaic interpretation and the new understanding given by Jesus, ". . . of old it was said to you . . . but now I say to you. . . ."

Even more than the specific areas of fulfillment of prophecy and law, the Gospel attests to the messianic mission of Jesus in its reporting of His daily-life events.

Reminiscent of Yahweh's total dominion over all creation described in the book of Genesis, Jesus repeatedly asserted a divine role by His mastery of this same creation's elements and life. Storming seas and winds obeyed His command; water sustained His physical weight as He walked upon it; water turned into wine at the sound of His voice; bread broke the bonds of quantitative limitation so that small amounts multiplied to feed large crowds; commonplace things such as spittle, dust, a look, a touch under His guidance reversed the course of disease and suffering, restoring health to troubled bodies; merely by His willing that it be so, victims of death came back to life and evil spirits were dispelled.

The Gospel authors record the jurisdiction which Jesus exercised over rights which are properly God's alone. Sin, an offense against God and therefore forgivable only by God, was forgiven by Jesus; the terms of the "your God—My people" covenant were altered and ordered by Him, as were the regulations pertaining to God's reserved day of worship; Jesus took upon Himself the role of eternal rewarder of good and punisher of evil.

The Gospel recounts occasions when Jesus made use of knowledge which belonged to God as a proper attribute. He foretold the contingent future in detail as it pertained to Himself, to other persons, to the nation, to material things; the secret thoughts and motivations of friend and foe were known to the mind of Jesus and He exercised the right of revealing these things; the plan and means of salvation whereby the salvific will of God would be fulfilled were decreed according to the mind and preference of Jesus.

The underlying point which gives essential meaning to the Gospel notation that Jesus fulfilled the law, performed miracles, forgave sin, foretold the contingent future is that He did these things in His own name and on His own authority. Sacred history is not lacking in examples where other persons engaged in similar activities. Even modern-day religious practices duplicate many of these functions. But between these activities, whether in the past or on the contemporary scene, and the same acts as performed by Jesus is so radical a difference as to accent the uniqueness of Jesus' mission and the commonplace aspect of all the others. Innumerable men have been chosen by God to exercise His power as His agents, but Jesus alone exercised this power on earth by His own right.

When Jesus spoke of the new law He did not draw His credentials from Moses or the national tradition as did the Pharisees; "...it was said to you of old, but now I say...." And in these words He placed Himself above and independent of the religious leaders and Moses himself. Yahweh had pre-ordained the law given to Moses, and Jesus pre-empted the Mosaic law, thereby equating his legislative right and authority with that of Yahweh Himself. This radical difference was not lost upon His hearers or the evangelists who recorded the reaction: ". . . the people were in admiration at His doctrine. For He was teaching them as one having power, and not as the scribes and Pharisees."

When Jesus exercised divine dominion over the elements, practiced the jurisdiction which is God's alone, used knowledge properly that of the Eternal Being, He never asserted, nor did His biographers suggest, that His performance was that of a delegate of God as all other historical figures were or are. Rather, the manner in which each of these powers was used, every time it was used, was distinctly that of a jurisdiction properly that of Jesus Himself.

This personal expression of proper authority by Jesus in matters precisely the area of divine operation is the key thought of the entire Gospel narrative. On this performance rests the credential which makes Jesus unique among all men, for thereby He displayed more than a human nature—He acted by virtue of a divine nature. Jesus manifested to those who would notice it that He, indeed, was a divine Person.

However, compelling as it is, the divine identification of Jesus was not left to innuendo or deductive reasoning from the writings within the Gospel books. Jesus attested to this reality in His own words and teachings. He asserted His superiority to Abraham, King David, and the Temple; the power over devils He attributed to His own dominion over the kingdom of evil; He preached the fulfillment of the prophets as having been accomplished in His person; He allowed without rebuke or correction the professions of His divinity made by the Apostles Simon and Thomas; He identified Himself as one with God. Finally, before Pilate, Jesus attested to His rightful claim to heavenly kingship.

The testimony of the Gospel to the divine activity of Jesus is clear and profuse. But the evangelists were not less effective in establishing that Jesus was a true human being, truly a man.

Jesus is clearly identified as the flesh and blood born in Bethlehem of Mary, a Jewish woman of the line of David, resident of Nazareth in Galilee. He was the subject of the religious rite of circumcision, fulfilled His obligations at the Temple ceremonials; He was recognized by His townspeople as one of their own; He was identified with the other members of His family clan.

As do all other human beings, Jesus suffered temptation from the evil spirit, enjoyed human friendship, experienced human emotions of anger, sorrow, love. His bodily existence was physically real, for He hungered, thirsted, tired, suffered. He moved around among people who saw Him, heard Him, touched Him.

The Gospel does not paint Jesus as an imaginary figure, an idealized fantasy, but as an authentic human being in an actual environment of time, place, and custom. The countryside through which He travelled, the towns in which He visited, the parables which He taught, the people who heard Him and their reactions to His words are all believable and in conformity with the scene of Palestine at the time of the Roman government. The Gospel does not exaggerate His acceptance or minimize His rejection, either as a Person or in the doctrine and practices He proposed. Thus the Jesus described in the Gospel conforms to the pattern of the Jewish mentality as the entire Old Testament presents it—Yahweh involved with His people in terms of real persons and events according to patterns proper to life-situations.

The Gospel portrayal of its central figure, Jesus of Nazareth, therefore, is the picture of a total human being—in every sense of the word, a *man*. As has been noted, this same source also identified Jesus as a possessor and exerciser of the divine nature. Adding together every detail presented in the first four books of the New Testament, the conclusion is inescapable—Jesus was truly God-in-flesh, the divine and human natures welded into the perfect unity of one Person. No wonder at all that this one figure stands in dominance of all history, unchallenged in impact, the essence of salvation's uniting of God and man in the covenant of love.

The two natures of Jesus present a formidable challenge to the Christian catechist. To overstress the divinity of Jesus is to isolate Him; to overstress His humanity is to destroy Him. While truly God, Jesus becomes brother to every man by sharing man's nature; but even while Jesus is truly brother, He transcends man at the divine level itself, for Jesus is the natural Son of God, therefore true God, while man is (through baptism) an adopted son, therefore only human. Catechesis must always maintain this balance lest the whole point of the Incarnation-Redemption renewal be lost—on the one hand in the non-relevancy of isolation and on the other hand in the familiarity of meaninglessness.

Finally, in keeping with the Old Testament manner and the Jewish understanding of Yahweh's providential and personal interest in His people, God's endorsement of Jesus is duly recorded by the evangelists. From the heavenly pronouncement of divine origin and holy nature made at His conception, through the messianic identification spoken by John the Baptist, to the heavenly proclamations at His baptism and transfiguration, the voice of God, so much a part of the Jewish religious experience, is quoted by the Gospel writers in verification of Jesus as a unique being, bearer of a unique mission.

Indeed, secondary only to these direct pronouncements, the miracles performed by Jesus constituted God's witness to

the verity of all that Jesus proposed in His life and in the salvific work He performed. And intrinsic to these proposals
and works was Jesus' claim to possession of both divine
and human natures. The "miracles and wonders and signs"
of which Peter spoke on Pentecost Sunday and so many examples of which the evangelists record in the Gospel biography
are God's seal of approval upon all that Jesus was and did
—union of God and man in one Person, renewal of all creation in the salvation of man through atonement for sin.

The unique work of Jesus was the revelation of God in
the fullness of Himself and the satisfaction for the sins of men
in His own death and resurrection.

The core idea in the Jesus revelation was the inner nature
of Yahweh—the triune God. The Chosen People knew Yahweh
only in His external manifestations (creation, providence, justice, mercy, and the like), and in this sense knew Him to be
one. But when Jesus revealed the inner nature of God (God
as He is in Himself), He demonstrated how that oneness in
the divine nature was possessed by three Persons.

Against the theological background of the Jewish people,
this was a difficult—indeed a repugnant—manner in which to
conceive the divine being, and the Jewish listeners resisted
the idea. Essentially, it was this resistance which formed the
excuse for destroying the propounder of the idea—a precedent
already provided within the law, namely, the death penalty
for blasphemy. It was this same attitude which dictated a
gradual unfolding of the mystery from veiled suggestions at
the beginning to clearer statements at the end; any other course
would likely have terminated Jesus' ministry before it was
barely launched.

The Jewish resistance to a concept of Yahweh which was
expressed in any sort of plural form is not hard to understand.
There is not a shred of evidence in the Old Testament to
indicate a trinity of Persons; any effort to find trinitarian
suggestions there can only be by looking back from the revealed fact—knowing the mystery of the Trinity, then reading
trinitarian interpretation into Old Testament texts. Also, the
idea of oneness always associated with Yahweh was a primary
distinction between the God of Abraham's followers and the
multitude of gods worshipped by the nations surrounding the

Chosen People. To suggest some sort of plurality in relation
to Yahweh was to equate Him with the gods of the pagans,
and this the faithful Israelite could not do. It was for just
such practices that the Yahweh-sent prophets had reserved
their strongest condemnations. It never occurred to the Jewish
mind that Yahweh could be Trinity in Unity.

In the teachings of Jesus as recorded in the Gospel, the
mystery of the Trinity is not presented in the technical, theological terminology with which later study and formulations
clothed it. The mode of presentation of the Gospel is informal,
whereas theological formulae are technical and precise explana-
tions. The Gospel (especially as written by Matthew, Mark,
and Luke) presents ideas which later are probed for meaning
and formalized in doctrines, somewhat in the Gospel according
to John and in the epistles of Paul, more so in the writings of
the Fathers and theologians of the Church.

Jesus' revelation of the Trinity followed the same pattern
as the Old Testament revelation of Yahweh—to express eternal
truth in the language of temporal happenings, to convey the
technical in commonplace terms. The audience which heard
Jesus teach was composed mostly of average people, not trained
philosophers or theologians; it was for the understanding of
this type of hearer that the mode of delivery was designed.

In this sense, the entire Gospel is a revelation of one
divine nature possessed by a trinity of Persons. The whole
concept of Jesus as the Messiah, His relationship to the prophets and the law, His exercise of divine prerogatives in His own
name and by His own authority; the authority He claimed
over salvation, angels, men, over the Temple and the patriarchs
bears a relationship to the traditional idea of God held by
His compatriots. Yet the manner in which these powers were
exercised established also a distinction between Jesus and the
Father. Taken together, the implication was clear: Jesus and
the Father are one and the same, yet they are distinct from
each other. From both text and context "Father" unequivocally
means "God"; the oneness, then, is in divinity, the distinctiveness is in Person.

This same theme is reinforced by Jesus' use of the term
"Father" in His reference to God and Himself, for the usage
is different from the manner in which He relates the Father

to the audience or to mankind. Similarly, the meaning conveyed by the phrase "Son of God" is not in the same sense
when applied to Himself as it is when the Gospel attributes
the title to other men

In addition to establishing an identity and a distinction
between Himself and the Father, Jesus speaks of a Holy Spirit
who likewise is identified within the divine concept but is
neither the Father nor Jesus. This Spirit will perform a similar
"advocate" function for the Apostles after Jesus leaves them,
as Jesus Himself did when He was with them; the Spirit will
be the rudder of truth and lamp of enlightenment which
proceeds from the Father, and will be sent to the Apostles by
the Father and by Jesus jointly.

The overall teaching given by the four evangelists, based
on the authority of Jesus, in their writing of the Gospel is of a
central figure who is identified in three different functions,
one God, three divine Persons—Father, Son, and Holy Spirit.

To believe that the Gospel teaching does not substantiate
the mystery of the Trinity is to deny the evidence from the
aspect of Jesus' immediate audience as this, too, is contained
in the Gospel books.

If the full implication of Jesus' trinitarian teaching was
lost upon the general audience to which He delivered it, His
teaching, actions, and mannerism clearly indicated to them
that He was, at the very least, some sort of an extraordinary
person. They identified Jesus with the greatest of the prophets,
saw in His presence a visitation from heaven, clamored to have
Him as their national leader. But to the more perceptive of
Jesus' hearers, and especially to those versed in things theological such as the priests and the Pharisees, the multiplicity
in the Godhead contained in His message was clearly perceived.

When Jesus forgave sins and established the fact by a
physical cure, the power by which He did these things was
immediately questioned; His identification of Himself as the
fulfillment of Isaias' messianic prophecy, His claim to prec-
edence over Abraham, His self-identification with the Father,
His denial of diabolic power and counterclaim to divine power
—all these and other similar instances brought charges of
blasphemy against Jesus and even efforts to stone Him to
death, as the law said a blasphemer deserved. At His trial,

when He openly replied that He was truly the Son of God, the high priest accused Him before the populace of the capital crime of blasphemy.

It was not only that Jesus was equating Himself with God that brought these serious and violent reactions; deeper than that, it was that Jesus was proposing a plurality in the traditional concept of God. It matters not whether this multiplication was by two persons or three or, for that matter, by even a greater number. Jesus was accused of divine multiplicity and for that, finally, was apprehended and executed. That Jesus taught that the number of Persons was three (as noted in our previous paragraphs) was incidental at the time—it was for teaching a number other than one Person. Therefore the Gospel witnesses, on the evidence of His hearers' reaction, that Jesus taught multiplicity in the Godhead—a multiplicity which we recognize as the Trinity of Persons in the Unity of Divinity.

In this great revelation the Christian beholds the eternal, perfect activity of the inner life of God—His very nature itself. This is a knowledge above the power of the human intellect to achieve by its unaided self, a knowledge able to be given only by one who Himself would know of it. Only by supernatural faith, through the revelation of Jesus, can man know of God's intimate life, and for Jesus to reveal it, He must already have known it Himself—which, precisely, is what He claimed!

This inner activity of the Godhead is the Father eternally and intellectually generating the divine idea of self, the consubstantial Son; the Father and the Son, from their mutual love for the divine nature, spirating love personified, the Holy Spirit. Each Person co-eternal, co-equal—that is, each Person is God. Attributed to the external activity of creation, the Father is creator, providence; the Son is Wisdom Incarnate, the redeemer; the Holy Spirit is love, the sanctifier.

In a beautiful though quite inadequate analogy, the mystery of the eternal, uncreated Trinity finds expression in the created, finite order of family society: the intense love of husband for wife and wife for husband draws both into so intimate a union that they actually become one in the flesh, producing from their love-union a new person; each family

member thereby lives in the unity of the same nature even
as each is a distinct person.

The second aspect of the unique work of Jesus was the
satisfaction for the sins of man accomplished by His own
death and resurrection.

The Gospel reveals that divine love poured itself out in
the form of the second Divine Person of the Trinity uniting
Himself to true human nature, and that this God-man sacrificed Himself in order to demolish the barrier human sin had
erected between God and man in the order of eternal union.
"For God so loved the world as to give His only-begotten Son,
that whosoever believeth in Him may not perish but may
have life everlasting."

Jesus made clear in His own words that His purpose on
earth was to fulfill the prophecy-promise made by God to
humanity countless centuries before in the Garden of Eden
at the birth of sin when God addressed the tempter: "I will
put enmities between thee and the woman and thy seed and
her seed. She shall crush thy head and thou shalt lie in wait
for her heel." Jesus summed it up, "For the Son of Man is
come to seek and to save that which was lost." And again,
"For I came, not to call the just, but sinners." And yet a
third time, "For God sent not His Son into the world to judge
the world, but that the world may be saved by Him." It was
man's rebellious will which separated him from God; it was
Jesus' obedience which reestablished the life of intimate friendship.

As has been mentioned earlier in this chapter, the messianic credentials of Jesus as the Savior are clearly recorded
in the pages of the New Testament's Gospel. The various
signs by which the Messiah would be known and by which
the messianic mission would be accomplished had been set
down in the Old Testament and were realized in the Person and
history of Jesus as recorded in the New Testament.

In Jesus' redemptive action were fulfilled also the covenants and the prefigures which had formed so vital a part
of the story of salvation history as this sacred narration looked
ahead to its climax and central figure.

The covenant with Noah, that upright man who was saved
from the destruction of the flood through the instrumentality

of the ark, found fulfillment in the salvation from eternal destruction wrought by Jesus in the sign of the great catch of fish brought into the boat of Simon Peter. This gathering into the boat would be carried on across the long sea of time in the new ark, the Christian Church.

The covenant with the family of Abraham, which was tested as Isaac carried the wood to the hill where he was to be slain by his father, was proven in Jesus. Jesus carried the wood of His cross to Calvary for the sacrifice—this time not to be stopped—by which the Son gave His life in obedience to the Father.

The covenant with Moses, whereby a People of God was established as a nation, was exhibited by Moses' overcoming the evil designs of the Pharaoh and was established by the law given to him on Mount Sinai. Jesus overcame the evil design of sin which separated man from God and thereby constituted a new People of God that would know no national or geographic bond. This new race of Chosen People was established in the fullness of the law of love which found total expression on the Mount of Calvary.

To complete the circle, the fall of all humanity in Adam and Eve, through the infinite merits of Jesus became the elevation of individual humans by their religious commitment to God; the disobedience of Adam which perverted the order of religion was overcome by the obedience of Jesus so that the violated rights of God were restored; the earthly bliss of Paradise which was forfeited by sin was once again obtainable in the heavenly joy of the saved. The primordial, intimate God-and-man relationship of the Garden was re-established in the blood of the God-man.

The messianic figures of the Old Testament move from their realm of shadowy types to full, living reality in the redemption accomplished by Jesus.

Joseph of the book of Genesis, by virtue of the betrayal engineered by his brothers who sold him into slavery, was raised up by God to save his own family from the physical hunger of the famine. Jesus, betrayed by His trusted Apostle into the hands of the persecutors and abandoned by His brethren in the hour of danger, was God's providential gift by which every generation could be the family of God. Through the unhappy treachery of a friend, Jesus would feed His brethren with the heavenly food which would save them from the eternal spiritual starvation of separation from God.

Melchisedech, priest and king, blessed Abraham and praised God on his behalf by the offering of the symbols of bread and wine. The eternal High Priest and King of history, Jesus, blessed the new descendants of Abraham and offered to humanity an unending sacrifice of praise which it could render to God when, under the signs of bread and wine, He endowed His people with His own body and blood as a constant renewal of His redemptive death.

The Passover lamb, through whose blood God's elect were saved from the death wrought by the avenging angel upon the first-born of Egypt, in Jesus, the "Lamb of God" who freely shed His own blood, became the first-born into the new life by which the angel of evil was frustrated in his quest for spiritual death. God directed that the Passover sacrifice be perpetuated through time as a memorial of His providence; Jesus decreed that His death be projected throughout all time in an unbloody sacrifice as a sign of His infinite love.

The exodus by which Moses led his followers through the waters of the sea from the physical captivity of Egypt, along the danger-ridden journey of the desert, to the "milk and honey" of a national homeland was lifted beyond time and place by Jesus. Through the water flowing from His pierced side into the sacrament of baptism, Jesus delivers His faithful from the spiritual captivity of sin; through the ministration of His Church He guides man along the sin-ridden path of life to the fullness of joy in an immediate union with God in the heavenly Promised Land.

King David, who united the tribes of Israel into one earthly kingdom and ruled them as their king, was fulfilled by Jesus, who united all the nations of the earth into one Kingdom of God and rules them forever as Lord and King. King Solomon, known for his worldly wisdom, builder of the beautiful Temple wherein Yahweh lived among His people, was but a faint preview of Jesus, whose revelation gave mankind knowledge of heavenly wisdom and provided the means whereby God would dwell in human souls, making them living temples of the Triune God.

The Gospel reminds its readers that the entire life of Jesus was salvific. From the moment divinity humiliated itself by uniting with humanity, redemption was a fact.

Thus on the day of Jesus' birth, heaven announced His title and mission, "For this day is born to you a Savior, who is Christ the Lord." At His presentation in the Temple, Simeon saw Him and proclaimed, "...my eyes have seen Thy salvation which Thou hast prepared before the face of all peoples." At twelve years of age, in the Temple, Jesus informed Mary and Joseph that He was already about His Father's business. At the river Jordan His precursor pointed Jesus out to the multitude in the salvific phrase, "Behold Him who takes away the sins of the world!"

But the redemptive act is generally conceived in its crowning manifestation and pictured as the great trilogy of the Last Supper, death on the Cross, and resurrection from the tomb.

The evening He was to be arrested and put on trial, Jesus and His Apostles were together for the annual celebration of the Passover meal. In the course of this ritualistic supper, Jesus took some of the unleavened bread. Looking to the Father, Jesus prayed, blessed the bread, broke it and gave it to His Apostles to eat. He performed a similar ritual with a cup of the meal wine. This performance altered the traditional pattern of the meal and thus drew the attention of the Apostles. But more striking to them were the words with which Jesus climaxed each of these singular ceremonies: "Take and eat, for this is My body. . . . Take and drink, for this is My blood."

Some time before this evening—perhaps a whole year—Jesus had plumbed the depth of the Apostles' faith. At Capharnaum He had told them and a multitude of His followers that He would give them Himself as a food, that they must eat of Him so that they might have life everlasting. Many of the multitude were unable to rise to the heights of faith this promise demanded and they no longer remained disciples. On that occasion, Jesus challenged the Apostles directly—either they would accept this proposition as true and within His power to bring about, or else they, the chosen ones, should also depart from His company.

Now at the Passover table this scene was refreshed in the memory of the Apostles, the promise of such a great mystery of faith flashed once again within their minds. Eat, drink—My body, My blood—these words fulfilled the promise. Here before them was the real Jesus living under the appearance of bread and wine, and they were literally eating and drinking of the living Lord.

Jesus had said another phrase in His Last Supper fulfillment of the Capharnaum promise—by way of explanation He added: "My blood of the new and eternal testament which shall be shed for you and for many unto the remission of sin."

The covenants of old, written in the blood of animal sacrifice, temporary, subject to cancellation, limited to one place and one people, were signs of retribution for the crime of infidelity to Yahweh; but now Jesus writes in His own blood the new covenant before the eyes of His Apostles, a covenant never to end because it would be constantly renewed unto the end of time, to embrace all men who would come to it in repentance, a cause and means for annihilating the sins of mankind.

The unique events of this last of Jesus' Passover meals looked forward to the future: to the morrow when the sign of this evening would be seen in the reality of His body and blood separated in the death of the Cross, to the countless tomorrows when this sacred, sacramental action would be repeated until Jesus would come again—"Do this in commemoration of Me . . . for as often as you do . . . you shall show forth the death of the Lord until He comes again."

On the next day, after a night of trials and terror, Jesus was led outside of Jerusalem's gates, up to the summit of Calvary, and there, together with two thieves, suffered the death of crucifixion. By this immolation, He expiated the sins of the world and satisfied the violated rights of His heavenly Father so that once again man could stand eligible for the everlasting God-union for which he had been created. On the Cross Jesus was lifted up so that a sinful world could gaze upon its redeemer. His head was bowed that He could look upon the men for whom He died. His arms were outstretched to embrace all of mankind in the supreme gesture of divine love.

The Catholic catechist finds a crucial standing point at this convergence of the Last Supper and the Crucifixion. For if it is true that the Holy Eucharist summarizes Christian doctrine and is the keystone of Catholic faith, then the authenticity and true perspective of the Christian catechesis must emanate from a balanced understanding and presentation of the mystery which is expressed in a food to eat and a sacrifice by which its eating is made efficacious.

The Passover meal which Jesus ate with His apostles that last night of His life was but one in a centuries old procession of commemorative suppers ordered for His people by Yahweh in memory of their divine election. But it was also the last one, for a new election and a new sign were about to come into being and the course of salvation history would go in another direction because of them. As a sign of that change, Jesus altered the meal ritual to include the changing of bread and wine into His body and blood.

Two points vital to valid catechetics must be grasped and clearly expounded by the catechist from this change in direction.

While the Last Supper with its eucharistic meal and the death of Jesus on Calvary were two separate events in time, they are theologically of one and the same order. The evening words of Jesus over the bread and wine constituted a sacrificial action in sign—the sacrificial action which was to be seen in its stark reality but a few hours later on the blood drenched Cross. In the Holy Eucharist, the sacrificial death cannot be separated from the consecrated species for they are one and the same truth. The Holy Eucharist of the Passover meal *was* because the death on the Cross *would be*. The meaning and import of the meal is rooted in the fact of the death, and the separate consecration aspects of bread and wine identifies the sacrificial separation of body and blood.

The mystery and the receiving of the Holy Eucharist by the Christian cannot be divorced from the death which Jesus underwent. Even though in temporal perspective it is possible to receive the Eucharist without renewing the sacrifice (as in the case of Holy Communion given in home or hospital), or to participate in the renewal of the sacrifice without partaking of the Eucharist as meal, in view of what Jesus said and did it is not possible to conceive the meal without the sacrifice.

The Eucharist ought to be eaten and the efficacy of eating it is because the sacrifice which confects it (the Mass) is the perpetuation throughout time of the sacrificial death of Jesus from which the first Eucharist sprung and to which every successive Eucharist looks back. This inseparable connection between the meal event and the sacrifice of Jesus' life on the Cross is a dogmatic fact and the most solid argument against "inter-communion" with Christians of other persuasions who do not share this essential note of doctrine.

Seen in this perspective, the reception of the Holy Eucharist is primarily a sign of oneness in belief and not merely one of physical unity. Thus while Catholics hold that the reception of Holy Communion unites each one to Jesus through the substance of the Eucharist and one with another through a common table and food, it is false to conclude that the sharing of the Eucharist is a sign or means of unity when there is no common ground of belief as to its nature. In fact, indiscriminate sharing of the Eucharist with those who hold divergent concepts of its nature could well be a scandal and a stumbling block, as well as a deterrent to hoped-for unity in belief among differing Christians. The Eucharist is a meal, the meal of the new and eternal covenant; but it is so much more than a meal—it is a direct and inseperable witness to the covenant sacrifice!

An over emphasis on the meal to the detriment of the sacrifice, or conversely to exalt the sacrifice and overlook the meal leads to a second dangerous pitfall which the catechist should studiously avoid, namely, the failure to present faithfully the doctrine of the Real Presence in the Holy Eucharist. To confine eucharistic teaching to the action of receiving the meal —Holy Communion—would put all the emphasis on the human, immediate receiving of the species; to concentrate too narrowly on the celebration of the Mass as the sacrifice of Calvary long since passed would be a catechesis without a physical and intimate connection to the present.

Properly balanced, the doctrine of the Holy Eucharist adds a new dimension to both meal and sacrifice—the immediate, personal presence of the Lord after Holy Communion and also His abiding presence among His people even beyond the moments of Mass and Communion. Full grasp of the reality of receiving the living, entire Jesus in Holy Communion will inspire the recipient to more intense personal prayer and contemplation during those moments when Jesus is actually tabernacled within this individual human body and soul thus enriching the awareness of God's providential interest and love as well as intensifying the appreciation for His goodness expressed in so exalted a sign of covenant. From this, hopefully, a more respectful atmosphere before and after receiving Holy Communion will pervade recipient and congregation.

Also, the knowledge of the Real Presence of Jesus in the consecrated species can renew personal devotion to Him in the Holy Eucharist and add to the value of the church building as a Sunday meeting place the additional role of an honored place for private prayer, liturgical services other than the Mass, and paraliturgical exercises of communal piety.

The Catholic doctrine of the Holy Eucharist is, essentially, the doctrine of the Real Presence: that the incarnated, the sacrificed, the resurrected Jesus exists here on earth, now, and just as truly as He did almost two thousand years ago. Then He existed in physical presence, now in sacramental presence; but then and now one and the same reality - Jesus the God-man with His people. The covenant presence of Yahweh, in cloud, in pillar of fire, in "a special manner" at the Ark of the Covenant fades entirely aside this new covenant presence of the living God Incarnate. Unless this great truth be known, understood, and practiced, the central beauty and attractiveness of the Catholic faith and the greatest insight into the perfection granted by the heavenly Father to this new covenant of salvation history will be blurred, or unappreciated, or totally lost to the understanding of His people.

The catechist, standing between the table of the Last Supper and the Cross of Calvary must unite the eating of a meal and the enacting of a sacrifice by proclaiming with full emphasis the doctrine of the Lord's enduring Real Presence in the sacrament of His love.

The willing death of Jesus on the Cross was a vicarious sacrifice. Absolutely sinless Himself, Jesus could gain nothing for Himself—the merit of His supreme act of obedience to the will of the Father was totally on behalf of mankind. Because Jesus accepted God's will and conformed His own human will to it perfectly, the death on the Cross was a wholly free action done on behalf of others; it was, therefore, a true and perfect expression of love for every member of the human race.

A life which was itself and in its every action truly and sufficiently redemptive need not have been carried to the limit of human degradation and suffering as was the life of Jesus in His passion and death. Yet such an extreme was chosen to be a constant reminder to mankind of the wickedness of sin which caused such a heavy price to be paid for its negation, and the limitless love of God for man that this price was, in fact, freely paid.

The total concept of selflessness and love which Jesus in the redemptive act represents is beyond human comprehension, for the excellence of Jesus as Redeemer is itself beyond understanding. Because Jesus was truly a divine Person—the Second Person of the Trinity, God's natural Son—His every action was that of an infinite being, and therefore Jesus adequately satisfied for the infinite malice of sin. Because Jesus was truly a human being—the flesh, blood, and soul born from the womb of Mary—the acts of His body, intellect, and will were true acts of man, and therefore Jesus adequately represented humanity in offering restitution for sin.

But as the sacramental flesh and blood of the preceding evening looked forward for full illumination to the bloody reality of Calvary, so was the vicarious love-action of Calvary made glorious in the subsequent event of the following Sunday.

Jesus had truly died on the Cross. Those of the official Jewish hierarchy who had plotted his arrest, trial, and crucifixion, as well as the pagan soldiers of Rome who carried out the deed, witness to this fact in the Gospel's account of the crucifixion. The body was taken off the Cross, hurriedly prepared for burial (because the Sabbath was imminent, and the laws of cleanliness had to be observed), and placed in a sealed tomb.

When the Sabbath day was over, and a more permanent preparation of the corpse could be made, some followers of Jesus went to His tomb to complete the embalming process. To their astonishment, the large stone which sealed the burial place was moved away and the tomb was empty. The body of Jesus was not there!

The news of this unexpected turn of events quickly spread to the other friends and companions of Jesus. On that very day—the first day of the week—Jesus was seen personally and physically by various individuals and (excepting Thomas) by the Apostles as a group. The Gospel, the Book of Acts, and St. Paul record other meetings of Jesus with His followers on the days following.

The books of the New Testament which relate the resurrection and the encounters with Jesus following upon it convey the certainty held by these inspired writers that it was the same real Jesus whom they wrote about after as before His death. The resurrected Jesus was not a vision, a merely spiritual experience, a phenomenon brought about by group hope or expectancy. As a matter of fact, the evangelists humbly and honestly confess to the skepticism of the followers of Jesus concerning His resurrection. Despite the foretelling of the event by Jesus before His death, it was not His followers who expected Him to arise from the dead, but rather it was His enemies who anticipated it.

The post-resurrection Jesus described by the sacred authors was a real flesh and blood person doing real life actions. Jesus spoke to His Apostles, ate with them, had them touch Him for certitude concerning His physical reality. He conferred powers upon His Apostles and, it can be presumed, put the finishing touches upon the teachings which they would soon take out to the world in His name and with His authority.

The significance for the whole of Christian doctrine and faith which the corporeal resurrection of Jesus holds cannot be overstressed. Jesus Himself had designated this event as the credential and only sign of His messianic mission. St. Paul, consequently, rests the whole validity of the faith on the truth of the resurrection of Jesus from the dead, and the Apostles and their successors preached the resurrected Jesus as the key to the plan of salvation.

As the Last Supper looked forward to the next day's Calvary event, so does the resurrection look back to that same happening. And all three events, because they are aspects one of another, all look forward to the *parousia* when Jesus will come again and to the fulfillment of human life in the presence of the Father to which He leads His followers. The

Eucharistic food is the pledge of future glory to the pilgrims on the road of life; the vicarious death is the effective cause of reparation for sin and restoration to God-life; for these same pilgrims, the resurrection is the vindication that the end of the pilgrimage will fulfill man's hope for glorification and immortality. In the resurrected, glorious, living Jesus mankind is renewed in faith and hope.

With the completion of this great salvific drama, Jesus withdrew His physical presence from the realm of the world and assumed that fitness of place which properly becomes Him. Sacred Scripture records that Jesus entered into the heavenly company of the Father.

The ascension of Jesus into heaven is complementary to the resurrection, as both are aspects of the one mystery of salvation: the resurrection glorifies Jesus and the ascension places the glorified Jesus in His proper setting, namely, with the Father. The understanding of the early Christian community as to whether the ascension occurred at a different time than the resurrection and the manner in which it was accomplished (visibly or invisibly) is somewhat unclear. The essential note of faith (which is not changed regardless of the time and circumstances of the ascension) is that the glorified Jesus is with the Father: Jesus said it would happen and the coming of the Spirit was dependent upon it happening. The point of research concerns when the ascension took place, and in what way it was an observed, visible event.

As a sample, confining this passing observation to the Gospel only (excluding Epistle literature bearing on the point), the evangelist Luke in his Gospel indicates that the ascension took place following a discourse with the Apostles on the day of the resurrection; but the same author, in his book *The Acts* (fifth book of the New Testament) speaks of Jesus appearing to the Apostles for forty days between His resurrection and ascension. Was the Gospel a mere contraction, Luke intending to give the fuller story when he wrote *Acts*? Or, given the ascension on the resurrection day, did Luke mean to convey in *Acts* that Jesus made trips back to earth for forty days? Or was there a dropping or adding of texts by editorship in one place or the other somewhere along the line?

In John's account of the Gospel, Jesus sends Mary Magdalene, on the morning of the resurrection, to tell the Apostles that He was ascending to the Father. That evening John records the appearance of Jesus to the Apostles in the upper room. Did Jesus ascend and return the same day, or was His statement to Mary similar to the "go to the Father" idea He proposed after the Last Supper, so that what He said means He would be on earth *until* His ascension? The same John quotes Jesus as saying, "I go to the Father and you shall see Me no longer." Would this not contradict the idea of ascending and returning?

The early patristic literature and liturgical practices do not give a definitive answer to the question, either. However, as both theology and liturgy developed over the centuries, the accepted understanding proposed by the practice of the Church separated the ascension from the resurrection by forty days, and accepted the idea that the ascension was a visible event witnessed by, at least, the Apostles. It would seem, therefore, the better approach in basic catechetics, until the direction is officially changed, would be to follow the understanding set by faith and practice.

The great mysteries of supernatural faith which have been considered in this chapter form the essence of the entire Christian life of worship. Because Jesus was a really divine Person, by His own right possessor of the God nature, He is fittingly accorded the worship which He receives in the Christian community. And because this same Jesus, God-man, was possessor of a true human nature uniquely united with the divine, His body and all parts of it are properly the object of worship. In view of the role of Jesus as the redeemer of mankind and thereby the means by which man's reconciliation with God was effected, Jesus is correctly hailed and called upon as *the* Mediator between God and man.

The mystery of the Blessed Trinity underlies every concept and form of Christian worship: the Fatherhood of God is made the mode of human adoption into the divine life through the mediatorship of the Son, and the Holy Spirit effects in man the love which unites God and man in a saving union.

Holy Church directs official prayers and feast days as well as private prayers and pious customs to the triune God, and in likewise honoring the Son and the Holy Spirit, implicitly acknowledges and honors the Trinity of Persons.

However, the liturgy of the Blessed Trinity is most eloquently expressed in the celebration of Mass. The Preface recounts and praises the Father role of God-in-heaven in union with the voices of the heavenly court; the Canon perpetuates the Incarnation-Redemption mystery of the Son-made-flesh; the Holy Spirit, as the Sanctifier, hovers over the whole Preface-Canon prayer as He accomplishes the ultimate in sanctification —the conversion of the mundane offerings of bread and wine into the heavenly food of Body and Blood.

In the Mass, all of salvation history passes before the human mind in praise of the Blessed Trinity. The great figures of the Old and New Testaments and the living and dead of the Church are called upon to witness the highpoint of the sacred action—God Himself coming into the midst of His people in the body and blood, soul and divinity of Jesus. This most august worship action is properly summarized in the Canon's concluding words: "Through Him, with Him, in Him, in the unity of the Holy Spirit, all glory and honor is yours, almighty Father, for ever and ever."

This same liturgical celebration of the Mass perpetuates the supper-death-glorification of the Paschal Mystery. From this sublime renewal flows again into the human mind the goodness and mercy of God made visible most perfectly in the Word-made-Flesh who dwelt among men and renewed them in God. To this same liturgical source the sacraments, the worship rites, and private devotion look for their own dignity.

Thus man sanctifies life and its activities by joining them to the life and work of Jesus—in the mystery of the Trinity, through the perpetuation of the redemption.

*   *   *   *   *

Jesus told His Apostles that He would go to the Father; but they were not to be left as orphans. He would continue to be present with them, He would send from the Father and

Himself the Holy Spirit to witness to the truth, to enlighten them in the things of divine wisdom.

Fifty days after the resurrection, when the Apostles were gathered together in the upper room, a scene reminiscent of the calling of the people of Moses into a nation of the elect at Mount Sinai was enacted.

As had happened so long ago, God made His presence known by natural phenomena—then in thunder and lightning, now in wind and fire. The Holy Spirit was made manifest upon the head of each one present and dwelt in them as divine light and strength. As Moses of old after his contact with God came down from the mountain and proclaimed the covenant to the people, so also did these latter-day Moseses leave the sanctuary of the upper room and go to the assembled crowd to announce the good news of the new testament written in the Blood of Jesus, "and there were added in that day about three thousand souls." On the Pentecost, in the divinely inspired proclamation of the Apostles, the new People of God was begun, recognizable in the doctrine of the Apostles' teaching office, in the liturgy of baptism and Eucharist, and in prayer to the heavenly Father.

CHAPTER IX

"---My People"

The covenants God made with Abraham and his posterity were recognizable bonds which eventually identified God's people by nation, cultic practice, and theological principles. While individually free to comply with or to violate the terms of the pact, compliance or violation was normally looked upon as of the whole people—the nation was faithful to Yahweh and it was rewarded; the nation was unfaithful and it was punished.

Jesus came to fulfill the covenant by perfecting it, not to destroy its basic format. By expansion of the covenant scope, it would no longer be limited to one nation but would embrace every race of mankind. From one Temple site and the figurative worship forms of animal blood to cover sins, the new covenant would erect its altars wherever men were gathered, and would pay homage through the mediatorship of the Blood of Jesus which obliterates sin; rather than theological principles expressive mostly of legal formalisms, the new people would live in and by the spirit of love which Jesus revealed as the inner life of God. Each man would exercise that freedom of conscience, choosing to accept love and to love in return, or to reject and refuse. The more faithful the members were to the covenant spirit, the more vital the whole community of the Faith; the less faithful the individuals, the less effective the whole.

Perhaps the best insight into the perfected covenant is in the contrast of accent between the old and the new—the transcendence of Yahweh in the former, and the immanence of God-in-flesh of the latter. Yet the new covenant was not detached from what preceded it, for the coming of the Messiah did not end but fulfilled the role of a Chosen People. Jesus formed the indispensable link of continuity between the Chosen People of old and their history and the new People of God whose history is the personal mediatorship of Jesus on behalf of mankind.

The continuity between old and new is essential because salvation history is but one record, from creation's beginning unto the end of time when, in the second coming of Jesus, creation will have reached its goal—all things glorified in the glory of the risen Lord. Continuity with the "Old Testament era" is so intimate that neither new nor old would be understandable by itself; the meaning of salvation history lies in recognizing the unity between the before and after of the historical Jesus, and His role as provider of that unity in and through the community of people which He brought about in His Church.

The presence of God to humanity portrayed in the Garden of Eden episode of Genesis finds perfection in the unity of God and man in the one Church, for the rejection and destruction wrought originally by sin is overcome now by the community of salvation which is in but not of the world; as God saved His loyal people from the world's destruction through the ark, God now saves them from the storms of worldliness by His Church. The Chosen People of old were God's voice to the world, the locale of His special presence on earth, and the possessors of divinely given doctrine, law, and worship. Now God speaks, through Jesus, by the voice of His Church, to which has been entrusted the holy things of salvation and the creed, code, and cult authenticated by Jesus Himself.

The "new covenant" of Jesus, then, in reality spreads itself to men of all times, supplying justification for those who preceded Him in time as well as those who would come after Him.

God's dealing with man through covenant and the vein of unicity which runs through the Old and the New ought to bring the catechist to a more profound understanding of the Jewish-Christian relationship within the universal People of God. That the Christian dispensation is distinct from its Judaic predecessor is the taught and prayed doctrine of the Church: "...My blood, the blood of the new and everlasting covenant." But because the "new" and "everlasting" note of the Christian contract is by way of fulfillment and perfection, it cannot be opposed to that which it fulfills and perfects. Jesus described His own mission in this framework: "I have come not to destroy the law and the prophets but to fulfill them"; and the Mass canon reminds us that in the sight of God "Abraham [is] our father in faith." Indeed, Vatican Council II in its *Declaration on the Relationship of the Church to Non-Christian Religions,* indicates not a finality of termination in the fulfillment of the covenant but rather a continuing, divinely mysterious interflow between the two: "The Church, therefore, cannot forget that she received the revelation of the Old Testament through the people with whom God in His inexpressible mercy deigned to establish the Ancient Covenant. Nor can she forget that she draws sustenance from the root of that good olive tree onto which have been grafted the wild olive branches of the Gentiles . . . . Indeed, the Church believes that by His Cross Christ, our Peace, reconciled Jew and Gentile, making them both one in Himself."

In view of the common thread of covenant development from less to more perfect, from early promise to later fulfillment in the Incarnation-Redemption-Resurrection mystery of Jesus and on to eschatological perfection in the kingdom of heaven, animosity to Judaism is animosity to the roots and goal of Christianity itself. Historical, social, ethnic, or theological animosity toward members of the Jewish race is a negation and denial of Christianity and was duly deplored by the Fathers of Vatican Council II. While Christians do and must believe in the objective uniqueness of their "your God—

My people" relationship formed in the historical realization of Jesus as Messiah, they must also admit to a subjective validity flowing from the religious commitment in good faith of their Jewish cousins. As individuals are enlightened by God's grace, authentic membership in the salvific community is open to Gentile and Jew. Accordingly, the just quoted document of Vatican Council II puts on record as true Catholic doctrine that "...the Jews still remain most dear to God because of their Fathers, for He does not repent of the gifts He makes nor of the calls He issues."

Under the encouragement of Vatican Council II, biblical development and improved catechetics will continue to unfold the Father role of God relative to all men and the total embrace of humanity made by the arms of Jesus outstretched in redemptive sacrifice, and from this understanding a better existential Jewish-Christian relationship will emerge.

To the extent that this better perspective permeates the belief and practice of Christian and Jew, to that extent will the love and harmony proper to the theologies of each wipe out the disorders and hatreds which have too often marred earlier periods of Jewish-Christian history.

The Gospel and the succeeding books of the Bible sketch the form of the community identifiable with the redemptive work of Jesus. Emphasis is given to those who directly accept Jesus and His salvific message and to those beyond the limits of time who live in unending union with God. "He who believes and is baptized will be saved; he who does not believe will be condemned." Scripture and history record the institutions and development of an earthly community as a living witness, namely, a recognizable society of persons in the world. It is this aspect of the covenant people which is the pilgrim Church.

The teaching of Jesus about His ecclesial assembly is amply reported by the four evangelists and reiterated by the authors of *Acts* and the epistles; indeed, the rationale of these latter authors' works is the birth and growth of the earthly Christian society.

Jesus personally went about delivering the message of revelation to His compatriots. He spread His evangelical ministry over a period of time and different geographical locations.

Undoubtedly, because of this pattern, there were hearers who heard Him but once, others who were more frequently in the audience.

But also, Jesus selected certain individuals who would receive more complete exposure to Himself, His signs, and His words. These chosen ones, disciples and Apostles, were selected and trained; they were given functions to perform; their commitment in faith and their understanding of the messianic role were plumbed. From their group was formed organization and hierarchy. They were specifically commissioned to carry on the ministry after Jesus' physical departure. To this elite and to all the multitudes they would form in Jesus through their ministrations, the Holy Spirit was given that the evangelization would be proclaimed in truth and flower in sanctity.

The new nation of God's people would be called by the Father from every part of the earth's surface to a community of faith—a living body of believers whose bond of union is charity, the Holy Spirit its life-giving soul, and Jesus Himself its head.

The identification of self and followers is the most striking part of Jesus' teaching about the community called the Church. He mentioned it in parable, He promised it in power and authority. Jesus categorically taught the persecutor of Christians, Saul, the factuality of the unity which has Jesus as head and men as members, a lesson so well learned that the converted Paul made it the core of his Church concept. The Church is the visible sign of Jesus in the world.

As would be any living body made up of members and head and fulfilling a function in the world, Jesus described His Church in terms of its visibility, organization, and recognizability. Those who would be His members on earth would be as a sheepfold, a kingdom, a field of wheat, to mention but a few. This body would have visible leaders and rules of conduct.

But the formal explanation of the unique society of men which is the Catholic Church lies in its invisible component. As the human body combines a transient, visible, physical quality, and an immortal, invisible, spiritual quality, so too would the ecclesial body—visible and variable in its membership of human persons, invisible and immutable in the divine presence always and everywhere with it—Jesus, wisdom of God, the Holy Spirit, guarantor of truth. In this duality of principle, the sign-presence of Jesus imitates His physical presence—visible humanity and invisible divinity.

In the world to work upon the world, the Catholic Church can be fallible in the worldly aspects of its operation, for this is its humanity, but is unerring in the salvation aspects of its teaching office, for this is its divinity. So imbued with the divine presence is the teaching office of the Catholic Church that either its fallible or infallible areas teach authoritatively and command acceptance and submission by the members. This is one of the qualities which makes the Church truly "catholic," for if each man were to understand and to apply Church doctrine, laws, and rituals according to his own mind, wherein would lie unity-in-extension? The Church is truly a society, and the formal aspect of any society is authority. Thus membership in the structured Church rests upon acceptance of and obedience to its authority as expressed in the voice of rulers and the writings of laws as these embrace and support the teaching, governing, and sanctifying mission.

Thus it is of utmost importance to the members of the Catholic Church and to those outside membership that it be clearly understood, and that they act in accordance with the principle of identification of Church and Jesus. Jesus cannot be found on this earth outside the structure of His visible Church, for He does not exist in time (and this on His own word) anywhere else. The Jesus of history was one, and the Jesus projected through time until its end is one, a presence in—indeed which *is*—the organizational, recognizable means which He founded and commissioned, namely, the Catholic Church. To the degree that one knowingly and willfully disassociates himself from the means instituted by Jesus, to that degree does he cut himself off from Jesus.

The Church was designed to embrace and to direct people in the living of their life-situations. So that Jesus and the Spirit could also be a real and meaningful force in this pursuit, divinity united itself to humanity in the mystical union which is the Catholic Church.

In the *Dogmatic Constitution on the Church*, the Council Fathers of Vatican II teach that the earthly society of the

Church is the presence of Jesus in the world of every man in all times, a presence in which Jesus enjoys primacy over the members, and which makes the Church truly God's instrument of salvation. As Jesus came from God as sole Lord and Savior, so does the Church, which is Jesus, unite man and God in love and service. Born into Jesus in baptism and nourished by Him in the Eucharist, the members grow in understanding of the salvific revelation and in union with God. In time the Church has the imperfections of the pilgrim; in eternity it will reach the perfection which is the goal of its pilgrimage—the Father, through the Son, in the Spirit. Here on earth the sign of the Church is the Cross because it is still in travail; in heaven, the glory of the empty tomb will be the emblem of the Church's fulfillment.

Essentially it is and must always be one and the same Church, for all men are subject to but one God and directed, therefore, to the one Mediator and Savior whom He has sent, Jesus. Insofar as man cannot save himself but is saved through God's grace given in Jesus, God's salvation is to be had here on earth by man meeting Jesus in His ecclesial presence.

The Church at its heavenly destination is the accomplishment of the divine will, brought about through the cooperation of the human will with God's instrument of salvation, the Catholic Church. Then perfected and glorified, the heavenly members form not a separate or distinct community of faith from the pilgrim brethren but a new dimension of divine life.

Sacred Scripture gives the seeds of two aspects of the one Church here on earth—a vertical view portraying a hierarchy of function and state of calling, and a horizontal view which pictures the scope of membership. Being a vital organism living in a variety and impermanence of times and situations, these seed forms have grown and developed in an atmosphere of expanding applications and understanding. The Church is ever a mystery, never to be comprehended; yet by study and observation it is constantly to be more deeply probed.

In the study of the hierarchical structure, time has unfolded the fullness of the role of Peter as foundation of the Church and its supreme visible head. Jesus established among His Apostles and their successors an office of primacy in which He placed Peter and which each of Peter's successors has inherited. To the holder of this office Jesus promised immunity from error in those things pertaining to the essential message of salvation, authoritative power in the ordering of the Church, and constancy of witness unto the end of time.

The apostolic body of eleven lives in the Church in the conglomerate of its successors, the whole body of bishops. In this group for the whole Church, and in his own jurisdiction for each of them, the bishops exercise the power given to the Apostles by Jesus to teach, govern, and sanctify the faithful.

As the Bishop of Rome is the successor of the Apostle Peter, so is the body of bishops the successor of the eleven Apostles. The power and function given to the Apostles, to teach, govern, and sanctify, is the proper power and function of their bishop-successors in a ministry of service to the whole body of the Church.

Even as the office of primacy established upon Peter was to endure until the end of time, so was the apostolic office in the person of his successor, and both in identical form. What Peter in his office was to his fellow Apostles, so the Pope is to his fellow bishops. Thus the Pope is a sign of the unity, and the college of bishops a sign of the catholicity, of the Church in its salvific role. The individual bishop, exercising the teaching, ruling, and sanctifying power proper to the episcopacy in a jurisdiction designated by the Supreme Pontiff, forms a bond between the universalism and the localism of the Church.

From this selected and authorized teaching and governing body, divinely charged with the responsibility of serving mankind in the matters of salvation, it is seen that the Catholic Church alone in the history of the Christian era is the fulfillment of the mind and will of Jesus. Other communities of religion are called churches because of their external resemblance to the one and authentic Church.

Under the jurisdiction of the bishop, the priest, differing from the bishop in power and in jurisdiction, ministers as the bishop's assistant where and how designated by the bishop, and for the well-being of the Church by virtue of the ministry flowing from the power of Orders.

Religious men and women bind themselves by vows to pursue the way of perfection in a state of life especially dedicated to the service of the whole Church through the corporal and spiritual welfare of its members. The common life lived and shared in the name of Jesus by innumerable religious is a living and powerful sign of the unity of the Church.

The laity sanctify their lives and life-activities by uniting themselves in and to the Church through participation in the sacramental life, by sharing with the hierarchy the knowledge and experience of worldly things which the lay state of life particularly possesses, and by giving witness to the world through lives of Christian commitment and God's universal call to salvation.

The scope of membership in the Church gives a horizontal picture of varying participation in the work of salvation, a picture of Christian existence and discipleship which looks forward to the end of time when the Church will have reached perfection and full unity. In the New as in the Old Testament, God's involvement with man is in a communal manner. Before the Messiah, the elect community was a preparation for the manifestation of salvation in a chosen people who would accept the Savior and would then serve as a magnet to draw all mankind to the fruits of redemption. The catechetics of the Church must avoid what has been a tendency at times in the past, the error of overaccenting erratic individualism or arbitrary absolutism as aspects of the Church. The Church is community, and, while it is to rule, it also is to serve. The sign of the People of God in the world is a family in service to each other and to the populace around it.

Ministerial and lay members together constitute this new People of God because all share in the kingly, prophetic, and priestly office of Jesus, even though the hierarchical and lay priesthood are essentially different. In the manner of concentric circles, the inner core of the People of God comprises membership in the divinely instituted, visible Church where commonness in sacraments, creed, and community forge a bond of unity. From this center and source flow out elements of sanctification and truth. Baptized Christians lacking in some degree or other the sacramental, creedal, community bond and thus outside the divinely instituted, visible Church, through their conformity to Sacred Scripture and true religious zeal, are in that manner joined to the Catholic Church and it to them; non-believers in the Gospel who nevertheless know part of God's truth through incomplete possession of divine revelation are related to that extent to the elect race; men of sincerity who follow the good dictates of conscience as they know them but who are totally ignorant of the Church, its Gospel, and God's revelation can be moved by God's grace along the way of salvation, for they, too, as humans share in God's will that all men be saved.

The vision of the total membership in the Church is one of unity in Jesus and charity member for member. It is a picture of mutually complementary roles in which every member—visible, invisible, pilgrim, glorified, clerical, religious, lay—serves each other. The People of God incorporated in Jesus continues the Chosen Nation of the pre-Christian covenant; elevated and perfected through Christ's redemptive work, it journeys along the way to final exaltation.

Both its vertical structure and horizontal scope show that the Church is ecumenical by its nature and should have ecumenism as a pivotal characteristic. The unity of Jesus of which the oneness of the Church is a sign must be shown by the earthly Church acting with other groups of people in order that all mankind may be drawn together in the one truth of salvation.

In the Second Vatican Council *Decree on Ecumenism,* the warning is given that the division within the Christian body is especially contrary to the unity of His followers prayed for by Jesus and signified particularly by baptism and the Eucharist. At the different milestones in history when men separated themselves and led others into separation from the Catholic Church, such actions were blameworthy for those who perpetrated them. The blame for the damage done, however, is not the same for the descendants of the separatists. Therefore, in love and with zeal, the Church and its members find bonds of union with the separated members and must constantly seek to increase and to strengthen these common connections.

The members of the Church need better to know and to live their religious principles and to avoid false or inaccurate allegations regarding those outside the membership of the Mystical Body. All parties ought to enter into active investigation and interchange of their varying religious views so as to bring better understanding of the causes, effects, and reasons for division and separation; thus knowledge and charity will bring individuals and religious communities closer and hasten the day of unity in faith and morality.

Common worship, when such does not damage the external unity of the one Church but does serve to increase God's presence among the participants, can be a valuable tool in the search for oneness among disparate groups when done under guidance of episcopal authority. Other effective means toward true ecumenism come from better knowledge of religious principles, honesty in matters of religious belief and practice, intergroup discussions, and mutual civic and social activities by different religious communities.

True ecumenical spirit and activity exercised by Christian men of good will within and without the various denominations will, through God's grace, bring about the hope expressed by Vatican II that "as the obstacles to perfect ecclesiastical communion are overcome, all Christians will be gathered . . . into that unity . . . which Christ bestowed on His Church from the beginning."

Ecumenism and proselytism are two different things, as the Council Fathers point out. Yet the duty placed upon His disciples by Jesus to make His message of salvation known to all men is not thereby abrogated. Nor does true fraternal charity endorse an indifference to the neighbor's spiritual good. Thus the full Catholic teaching must be the Church's tool in all ecumenical activity, especially in the dialogue, neither burying nor compromising any facet of revealed truth. The Church's role and mission is and always will be to spread the entire Gospel message everywhere and to everyone. Ecumenism is not to eliminate or adulterate the truths of salvation, but rather to create the climate wherein the proclamation of the entire body of divine truth can more effectively take place and wherein receptivity to it will be more readily had.

The evangelical and salvific role of the Church is exercised in the world of everyday life events and situations. While the Church is timeless, it is very much involved with time; while it is not worldly, it is very much concerned with a place in the world. Jesus was a real, existing Person to His historic time and place; so must be His latter-day presence, the Church.

The people of Jesus' time were real people, and the flesh-and-blood Jesus was real to them; the mystical Jesus and its orientation cannot be less so.

To emphasize this point, Vatican Council II dedicated its longest statement to *The Church in the Modern World*. This entire document is an urgent call to the visible Church and to its members to become conversant with and involved in the religious, political, social, and economic problems of mankind and its societies, and to bring to bear upon secular activities the sanctifying effects and principles of the Gospel message.

Science and technology are reforming the structures of human living so as, on the one hand to bring man to a more perfected manner of earthly existence, but on the other hand to undermine spiritual values, disturb traditional patterns, and accentuate inequalities. Only the Gospel truth can give mankind and his progress the direction and the values which will enable men to enjoy that full destiny which combines temporal and eternal success.

It is imperative to the presentation of sound catechetics to bear in mind that the social gospel of the Church needs always to be the application or reflection of the salvific Gospel of Jesus, else the Church has lost its very purpose for being. Even as man must look sideways to see his fellowman and his needs, so must he be looking upward to see God. Unless God is seen as Father and fellowman as His child, in His image, and destined for eternal glory with Him, there is no motivating or enduring basis for human fraternity.

Religious guidance must sanctify politics, social conditions, and economics lest these things secularize religion. Thus the role of religion in the modern world is not that of the revolutionary who seeks only a pragmatic, here-and-now eradication of evil symptoms by whatever appears the most effective means. The Church as leader and its members as doers in the mission to the modern world must cure worldly ills by applying religious values to the roots of the disease. Then will the Church be a faithful witness to Jesus and an effective instrument of His philosophy, "Seek ye first the kingdom of God and His justice; then all other things will be added."

The Christian remedy for the ills which plague man and his world lies in the recognition of each individual person as a child of God, destined to live on this earth in a dignity befitting such a Fatherhood, and to share in the glory of it in the realm of heaven. Thus each man deserves the exercise of human freedom, pursuit of betterment, and a fair sharing in the bounty provided by God and the riches produced by man. Mutually assisting one another in the achievement of this goal, fellowmen, private and civil societies, and the Church will bring about the community of mankind as the family of God which salvation history, the life and message of Jesus, the structure of Church and state, and human nature itself reflect as God's design for His creature, man.

The Council teaching in the *Dogmatic Constitution on the Church* reminds the faithful that the Church finds its type and figure in Mary, the mother of its Lord, as she is identified with the physical body and the Mystical Body of Jesus. Mary is intimately associated with the Genesis promise of divine mercy and the conquest of evil—it is her Son, in His physical body and in His Mystical Body, the Church, which is the seed that did and does combat with Satan to restore mankind to fellowship with God. Mary is established in her dual maternity: physically, at the scene of the annunciation and the birth in Bethlehem; ecclesiastically, at the foot of the Cross where the projected Christ, the Church, was born. The faithful who would witness to Jesus as His disciples were represented at Calvary in the Apostle John. When Jesus bequeathed Mary to John and John to Mary, the figure of the future was established: the mother became mother to all the disciples to come, the disciples became children to her. "... there is your son, ... there is your mother." The pilgrim Church of the redeemed, at its sign of the Cross, was given relationship to the mother of the redeemer. She, as every member of the saved, was redeemed by the merits of Jesus, the one mediator, who established a direct union between God and the faithful; she, because of unique proximity to Jesus on earth and in heaven, constitutes a powerful intercessor and an efficacious patroness.

In Mary's womb God wed divinity and humanity into one Person, who in Himself and in His Church labors to unite God and man in sanctity and salvation.

In Mary's perpetual virginity, her sinlessness, and her glorification she so well represents the Church—integral in its faith, hope, and charity, elevating men from the life of sin to the practice of virtue, destined to be fulfilled when the redeemed stand body and soul before God in unending glory. In her free-will acquiescence to the divine plan of salvation, Mary was the pattern of the Church's continuing assent in faith to the message of the Savior.

The catechist must walk a careful line between under- and overemphasis of the role of Mary in Christian doctrine. Mary is meaningful in the context of the life of Jesus; she mothered His physical presence and continues to be the mother of His mystical presence, the Church. If proper bounds were exceeded by overemphasis in the past, the mistake will not be corrected by an underemphasis in the future. By God's choice and design Mary, the mother of Jesus, is unique in herself and her motherhood; fidelity to the mind of God acknowledges, honors, and rejoices in the prototype of the redeemed.

The whole idea of liturgical life and action is coextensive with that of the Church as the People of God, chosen but not yet glorified. Jesus is the mediator between God and man, praying and sacrificing to God on behalf of man, sanctifying and endowing man on behalf of God. The Church is Jesus existing in time for all time and for all men who will come to Him as Lord and Savior; the liturgy is the Church perpetuating Jesus' presence, the magnet drawing men to God in praise, petition and thanksgiving, and the nourishment whereby they grow in knowledge, love, and service of the Father through Jesus by the Spirit. Thus the action of Jesus is the action of the Church; when the Church acts liturgically in its salvific mission, it is Jesus acting.

The Second Vatican Council took note of the centrality of the liturgy to the Church and to Christian living in the *Constitution on the Sacred Liturgy*. It taught, in summary, that the liturgical life is a society living—the Elect of God of the new and eternal testament in the Blood of Jesus. It is only in the framework of the Church as a recognizable society that this communal life as a Chosen People can exist, give its witness, and be seen by mankind. The liturgy in its sacred sounds and symbols is the vital sign of the Church's presence in the world.

Supernatural faith is expressed both in adherence to the Church as the living Jesus in the world and in participating in those acts of worship which the Church prescribes to express that presence. Jesus acts through the assembly of His people in the liturgical rites, and in the same rites the faithful act in and through Jesus, as is manifest in the formulae of official prayer endings. Thus the unity of the Catholic Church which comes about through Jesus is exemplified by the union-in-action of the liturgy, pre-eminently in the celebration of His sacrifice in the Mass and the eating of His body in the meal of the Eucharist.

CHAPTER X

Response

The benevolence of God in covenant relationship with man is a freely bestowed demonstration of divine mercy and love. Acceptance or rejection of the proffered bounty is a free act of human response.

In the new covenant, man's response is a submission in love to the reality of a living Person rather than the expression of love through obedience to legal forms so characteristic of the Mosaic covenant. The terms of the new covenant are written in love acts of personal relationship rather than in precepts of human origin. Man's free response to God's covenant benevolence is either a positive action in that he returns love to the Lover, or a negative action in that he refuses to reciprocate divine love. The positive signs, love-giving, are made in worship of God and service of fellowman for God's sake; the negative signs, love-refusal, are made in the commission of sin.

Fundamental to both positive and negative reactions of man to God is the new life in the Father given to man through

Jesus and preserved in vitality by the Holy Spirit. As a fruit of the redemptive mystery, the human soul is destined to enshrine within it, and hence within the total person, the life of the Triune Godhead, and to do this by a free-will human act. The person who receives and increases this divine Presence responds positively to God's salvific message; the one who refuses or destroys the indwelling of the divinity responds negatively to God's gift of temporal and eternal union. No longer a testament of types and figures, the love-union of "your God—My people" is now a reality expressed in terms of life itself—divine life, human life.

The Gospel records this new dimension of human living as taught by Jesus.

Jesus assured His followers that He would not leave them orphans, alone. He would make His abode with them even though they did not directly experience the presence of His physical body. Nor would they possess Jesus only. The Father would be present with Jesus, and the Father would send the Holy Spirit—all three divine Persons thus making an abode in the members of the faithful who accepted Jesus by faith and served Him in love. This divine presence with the Church is a presence in the members, for the Church is its members.

Jesus spoke of the divine indwelling under various similitudes: He is the life-giving vine from which life flows into the member branches; He is the heaven-sent bread of life and the source of living water (the staples of life) so that the one possessing this bread and water will spring up to everlasting life.

The indwelling of the Trinity in each faithful member of the Church is explained by Jesus—that men "might have life and have it more abundantly."

Jesus' teaching concerning the life He would provide is the revelation of an available life higher in value than human existence, noble as that is. The hearers of Jesus' words, the ones to whom He made His promises, were, after all, very much alive with human life. To speak of giving life to the inanimate could mean the gift of life where it would not be due; but to promise life to those already living earth's highest form of natural life, and to say that the life to be given would be more abundant than what was already due and had, was to describe the gift of a distinctly different and higher order from what human nature should expect. Jesus taught that this endowment would be divine life itself: the Father, the Son, and the Holy Spirit dwelling in human persons—this was the source and the explanation of the more abundant life. Because Jesus lived the God-man life naturally expressed, men united to Jesus in faith and love could also live in their lives a pattern of this union. Man would not live alone, God would live in him.

Possession of this gift of divine life enables man to act in a manner beyond the capability of the merely human. The writers of the New Testament epistles express this higher power in terms of man's ability to choose or reject God as a partner in life's situations. In light of the choices made, man directs his earthly existence toward or away from perfected and eternal union with God, for by the power of this implanted God-life, man can transcend the human limitation of indirect union and achieve the supernatural level of a direct beholding of God. The renovation of human destiny consequent upon the gift of the divine life is seen in the contrast between the natural life in which man is born to sin and death and the supernatural life where birth is into the family of God with the promise of eternal existence with Him.

Thus the epistles reveal the condition brought about by the divine indwelling as one of true holiness, not merely an imitation of it. The soul in union with the God-life is a partaker of the divine nature, sanctified and justified by it, for such a person is transformed from the darkness of separation from God into the light of membership in God's family. This true conversion is as radical a difference as is that of death and life—God's life in a human person distinguishes between the natural death-in-sin and the supernatural life-in-adoption.

The life of God in a human soul is as truly a source of power as is natural life itself. The call to union in Jesus, the choice of good works, the identity as children of adoption are all concomitants of and presuppose the indwelling Godhead. It is God who works in man both as to his choices and his accomplishments.

There is nothing on the part of God whereby He is required to give His own presence to man—God is the perfect

Being, perfectly free. Nor is there anything on the part of man whereby that elevation above human nature is owed to him. Thus the indwelling divine life is in the purest sense of the word a gift.

The life of God given to men is a fruit of the redemptive mystery and a consequence of the covenant. Therefore, while the divine presence perfects and elevates human activity, it does not destroy human nature. Man is free to live by the covenant in the presence and power of God or to reject God's benevolence. The free will of man chooses the goal of life and the course to follow in reaching the chosen end. The supernatural power derived from God's indwelling presence enables man, if he chooses this end, to achieve sanctification in time and in eternity.

In the terminology of the Church, the above described indwelling presence of God in a human person is aptly identified as *sanctifying grace,* a gift which makes its receiver holy, and *actual grace,* a gift which inclines man toward holiness.

In the sanctifying and actual grace flowing out of the redemptive sacrifice of Jesus, man passes over from the bonds of sin forged in the Garden of Eden to the freedom of the children of God. The goodness of the original creation pattern is restored in the intimate friendship of God and man here on earth—a means and a sign of the perfected union in the eternal, promised land.

The God-life comes into a human soul principally through the sacred actions of the seven sacraments. These are the sensible signs which effect the transmission of grace and are also the indication to man that the gift has been received. The sacraments properly received are the highest order of the positive, love-giving worship signs by which man unites himself to God.

The more a sign resembles the reality it signifies, and the more intelligible the signified reality is made by its sign, the more true and effective the sign is. Thus the highest sign of God's covenant with man is Jesus Himself, by whom God is made visible to man in the humanity of Jesus and in the divine wisdom and power which Jesus made manifest. The most perfect sign of God's love for man is given by Jesus' redemptive action in which the sin barrier separating man from

God was breached. The clearest sign of God's fidelity to the new covenant of salvation is in the visible and recognizable Catholic Church whereby Jesus' ministry of reconciliation and sanctification is continued through the centuries. In this sense Jesus, redemption, and the Church are sacraments.

All three of these signs enter intimately and meaningfully into the life of a faithful follower of Jesus through the seven sacraments which Jesus instituted and His Church dispenses. Through these sacred signs is accomplished a meeting with Jesus in covenant; they draw their efficacy from Jesus in His redemptive act; they witness to Jesus' faithfulness in the sanctification of men through the ministry of His Church.

Each of the seven sacraments serves a distinct function in conforming a human existence to the pattern of salvation, and all the sacraments effect the man-to-God union which is justification. Therefore, while the ultimate goal of the sacraments is one—the God-life in a person as a pledge of future glory—yet the sign of each sacrament is different; thus each sacrament exemplifies the aspect of the God-life given by it and makes the identity of self-commitment wrought by that phase of divine encounter more clear to the recipient.

While modern catechetics emphasizes the sign value, and properly so, for the impact of the sign had too often been neglected in the past, it does not follow at all that the sign should overshadow the reality it signifies. The commendable effort to make the sign realistic and meaningful could happen at the expense of concern only for sign. As an example of this danger, the current effort to make the bread-sign of the Eucharist more "bready" and reception of this sacrament more distinguishable as a meal can cause the color, quantity, time, and manner of consumption of the species to be of more concern than the fact that what is being received is not bread at all but the Real Presence of the glorified Jesus.

Or, the sign of the sacrament of penance as a reconciliation of the sinner with the Christian community could lead to a degree of communal emphasis where individual revivification is overlooked.

Or again, the use of the sacrament of penance with too much accent on the psychological roots and manifestation of the sign can lead to ignoring the intensification of God-life

which each worthy and attentive reception of a sacrament produces. Children knowledgable in good and evil categories of
behavior with parents, playmates and in the classroom can be
equally aware of right and wrong conduct toward God.

In the light of this, it would seem that the contention of
some modern moralists and the practice by some modern
moralists and the practice by some present-day catechists that
children should be in the adolescent stage of life before receiving the sacrament of penance is groundless, even dangerous.
Indeed, such a course might well find a candidate for first
confession already deeply entrenched in a habit of sin and
psychologically indifferent to moral good and evil. The true
catechist ought to avoid substituting psychological theory (on
which not all psychologists agree) for moral principles and
practices which have been the universal teaching and tradition
of the Church and of its most renowned moralists for so long
a time.

A child intellectually mature enough to grasp, at least to
a minimal degree, the most profound mystery of the sacramental presence of the Lord in the sacrament of the Eucharist
must also be assumed to be mature enough to distinguish between penance and Holy Communion, so that the former is not
understood as a prerequisite of the latter (except in the case
of mortal sin, a very doubtful capability in a child) just because first confession precedes first holy Communion. An adult
responsible for only minor infractions, or free of any known,
wilful sin, can still profit by the salutary and strengthening
effects of regular, periodic reception of the sacrament of penance. Thus children and adults in the circumstances mentioned
and others which are similar ought not to be discouraged from
sharing in the good fruits of devotional confession just because
the sacramental "sign" may be less clearly expressed.

Even as the created humanity of Jesus placed man in
physical contact with God, so do the sacraments use created
things to place man in contact with Jesus. Thus things of
creation, once the instrument of man's separation from God,
are now the vehicles whereby man is renewed in the God-life.
Not only man, then, finds restoration and elevation through
the Incarnation-redemption mystery, but by inanimate creation's
sacramental role in the transmission of holiness, God sees the

whole of creation directed to Him and in this it is once again "good."

The sacraments return inanimate creation to the service of mankind as a sign of God's love—but now perfected, in that from a mere physical service to man creation becomes a spiritual tool. Love desires union and the good of the beloved. Insofar as the material signs of the sacraments effect the God-life in the human soul, they serve love's craving for union. Because the indwelling of God is man's greatest good, the materials of the sacraments, the instruments bringing this gift, satisfy love's desire for the good of the beloved.

But most noble of all, the sacraments bring human souls dispersed throughout time and in all places into a personal contact with Jesus as real, as efficacious, as that enjoyed by the persons to whom He ministered in His physical presence. This because Jesus is the reason for the efficacy of the sacraments; He is, through a human agent, the minister of every sacrament. Because it adopts a person into the family of God, baptism is an encounter with Jesus as a brother; confirmation empowers fitting witness to the message of salvation, and so in it one meets Jesus as the revealer; penance is the sacrament of contact with Jesus, the conqueror of sin and merciful reconciliator; the Eucharist is Jesus feeding the multitude with the bread of life; in the anointing of the sick, Jesus is met as consoler and encourager in times of crisis; Jesus the redeemer and mediator lives and acts through the sacrament of Orders; Jesus, united with humanity in the mystery of the Church, is encountered in the matrimonial union of spouses.

In bequeathing to His Church a ministry of sacred signs, Jesus was following a pattern used throughout the Old Testament and in His own preaching. In Yahweh's dealing with the Chosen People and in Jesus' proclamation of His messianic role, as in the sacraments of the new covenant, outward signs accomplished inner effects. The offering of sacrifices, the Ark of the Covenant, the ritualistic prescriptions of the Old Law; the use of bread, of spittle, of water and other mundane things for Jesus' performance of miracles in His time—these were indeed the signs and types which the sacraments, as purveyors of holiness itself, fulfill and perfect.

A full catechesis of the sacraments in the spirit of the new catechetics is an area all its own. Books have been written on the subject. An effort limited to orientation, as this present book is, cannot consider sacraments in detail. It must suffice here to note the New Testament's identification of the seven sensible signs which the Church holds to be the channels of God-life for the human soul instituted by Jesus.

Baptism, by which a man is born into the new life of the resurrected Jesus to become an adopted child of God and a sharer in the priesthood of Jesus, was taught by Jesus to be a requisite for eternal glory and He commanded His Apostles to perform the rite.

Confirmation brings that special presence and strength of the Holy Spirit which Jesus had promised and which was fulfilled on Pentecost Sunday for the Apostles, who then went out to lay hands upon the baptized.

Penance reconciles the sinner with the merciful God and the community of the covenant people by restoring the friendship destroyed through sin, or strengthens that friendship if no serious sin be present.

Holy Eucharist is the sacrament especially exalted, for it preserves the real presence of Jesus with His followers, renews the mystery of the Incarnation-redemption, and constitutes a bond of unity welding the faithful into one community in and of the Lord.

Anointing of the Sick brings peace of soul and the strength of resignation to God's will to those for whom death from sickness might be imminent.

Holy Orders specifically delegates certain men with the power of Jesus as priest and prophet, to march at the head of God's people, leading them to fulfillment in the word and the bread of the Lord.

Matrimony signifies the union of Jesus and the Church by sanctifying the lifetime bond between man and wife, even as Jesus made the water a more precious fine wine at the marriage feast in Cana of Galilee.

As God has chosen to express His covenant visibly in sacred signs, these same signs form man's most noble manner of making positive love-signs of response to the divine proposition. The shadowy manifestations of the "your God—My people" balance before the coming of Jesus gave imperfect witness to the providence of God and the allegiance of man. The response to the covenant was less meaningful and effective. The cultic rites symbolic of submission gave way after the advent of Jesus to signs efficacious of partnership. Jesus summed up the transition, "I will not now call you servants . . . but I have called you friends."

Legal incorporation into the nation of the Chosen People expressed by the rite of circumcision gave way to baptism in water and the Spirit, a birth into the very family and life of God and membership in His Church.

The anointing of kings and prophets of the Old Law as a sign of their ministry of witness to the presence of Yahweh was superseded by the coming and indwelling of the Holy Spirit in confirmation, that the Christian might inform the world by word and deed of his life-in-Jesus.

The symbolic ritual of divine clemency performed in animal sacrifice or the goat of propitiation became true man-to-God reconciliation through the Blood of Jesus in the sacrament of penance.

The lamb of the Passover and the bread of the manna nourished the bodies of the chosen race, but the food of the Lord given in the Eucharist vivifies man's soul in the Giver of the gift of life. The presence of Yahweh with His people signified in the Ark of the Covenant paled next to the Real Presence with the new elect in the Holy Eucharist.

The imperfect animal sacrifices of the Temple priesthood were elevated and transformed by the priesthood of Jesus in Holy Orders to confect the perfect sacrifice of the Lord's Body and Blood.

The natural union of man and wife established by God in the Garden was elevated to the supernatural, meritorious union of matrimony in the mystery of Jesus and His Church.

Although the Old Covenant had no prefigure of it (before Jesus, one could not go from this life into glory), the new dispensation has the sacrament of the anointing of the sick for spiritual strengthening in the final hours of pilgrimage.

The participation in the celebration of a sacrament, then, needs to be viewed as a piece in the mosaic of salvation history, moving the People of God along the way from creation to parousia, up from the sphere of the earthly to the horizons of heaven. No sacramental happening can be insignificant or routine—each is, and therefore ought to be entered into, as a magnificent display of divine love and human response. In each new entering into sacramental life, the divine encounter of Adam is re-enacted on a higher level; the personal call and involvement of the patriarchs goes out again to mankind, a human person steps further along the exodus from world to God. Every sacrament renews the Father's involvement with man through Jesus in the Holy Spirit by which the Temple becomes a human person alive with the life of God!

The sacraments are man's finest response to the divine love call. Every experience of sacramental ministration is a coming into a Person-to-person meeting with the redeeming Jesus, the sanctifying Spirit, and the providential Father—a pre-state to eternal, direct life with this identically same Blessed Trinity in heaven.

Another way in which man makes his positive, love-giving response to God's invitation to unity-through-indwelling is prayer.

In its broadest sense, every deliberate action of the Christian powered by the God-life can and ought to be a prayer, a direction of the human self to the will of God. The overall pattern of creation, as looked back upon from its glorious termination in eternity, will be seen as a great tapestry in which every human action added a thread to the design. The pageant of mankind's movement to God begun at creation in the Garden and continuing until the parousia is but a progression developed from human choices. Therefore the good that man does in this life praises God by completing the divinely conceived created pattern. Good works are prayers.

But in a narrower sense, prayer is a specific form of human action which honors God as supreme benefactor. Prayer is communication between God and man, a two-way exchange which unites both parties in a common interest—man talking (mentally, or mentally through speech) and God answering through grace and favors.

The Gospel draws a clear picture of Jesus as a man of prayer in word and action. He took part in the religious rites of the Jewish people, a worshipper at the Temple of

Yahweh. He undertook His public ministry only after an extended period of prayer, and interspersed His teaching years with retreats in the solitude of prayer. Jesus prayed with and for His Apostles, prayed in His dying moments on the Cross. In response to the request of His Apostles, Jesus prepared and gave them a model of the prayer life in the "Lord's Prayer."

Jesus commended to His followers a life patterned on prayer—to ask so that they could receive, to seek so that they would find, to knock so that grace might be opened to them. He promised efficacy to all prayers based on the mediatorship of His name.

The practice of habitual communication with God in prayer is a sign of response of trusting love to God's providential love, shown so specifically in the gift of His Incarnate Son as man's Lord and Redeemer. This love response to Love is made by the People of God as community and by persons as individuals; in either manner, it follows the pattern characteristic of salvation history.

God prescribed social-liturgical prayer for the Old Testament temple, and the Eucharistic prayer of the Mass and the liturgical rites of the sacraments for the New Covenant assembly. Of old, God's people intimately and individually spoke to Him in psalms and devotional prayers; now, in imitation of Jesus and patterned on the prayer He composed, people worship the Father by offering private prayer and pious devotions.

The new catechetics must assiduously avoid giving the impression that a dichotomy exists between liturgical (official prayer of, by, and for the community), and devotional (personal prayer of, by, and for the individual), prayer. Prayer itself is one—a communication of God and man. Man himself is one—a free, responsible person. But even as man has two aspects to his nature, that is, man is an individual and a social being, so, too, must his prayer have two faces—liturgical, communal prayer of a society with Jesus at its head, and devotional, individual prayer of a person-to-person relationship to Jesus as brother. The Christian ought to balance these two forms of prayer in order to relate to God the two needs of his nature.

Yet a distinction in hierarchical value does exist between public, liturgical prayer and private, devotional prayer. In its *Constitution on the Sacred Liturgy,* Vatican Council II teaches that ". . . every liturgical action . . . is a sacred action surpassing all others. No other action of the Church can match its claim to efficacy, nor equal the degree of it. . . . The spiritual life, however, is not confined to participation in the liturgy. The Christian . . . must also enter into his chamber to pray to the Father in secret."

Prayer enjoys an exalted place in human activity because it is an occupation of the total human. In acknowledgment of God as creator, sustainer, and source of all things, man places himself in prayer relationship to God by involving his whole self in worship, adoration, thanksgiving, and petition. Prayer accomplishes this end: it involves the intellect in a truly intellectual activity of contemplating God, brings the will to a free choice of God as the object of its action, stirs the emotions of peace and love by association with God, and uses bodily members and organs to accomplish the spiritual movement to God—the whole person prays.

The Mass is the prayer *par excellence* and proximity to it measures the efficacy of all other prayers. In every Mass the entire Church as the People of God renews the covenant to which it witnesses in the world, the covenant in the redemptive action of the Lord. The Mass has the same victim, priest, and purpose as Calvary; therefore it is the most perfect sacrifice and the most noble of all possible human acts. The Mass confects the same food of the Lord's Body and Blood as was done in the upper room, and offers this most noble meal so that all men might be united with each other and made one with Jesus in the bond of covenant love. The Mass brings about the glorious presence of Jesus as signified by the abandoned tomb so that in sacramental form He is present with His people for all time, that they might not be in the world as orphans.

Jesus taught how the way to human union with the Trinity by means of divine indwelling is through conformity of the human will to the divine will, by love of God and love of neighbor. Indeed, in service to fellowman Jesus measured the extent of love: "Greater love than this no man has, that he lay down his life for his friends," and "Whatsoever you did to the least of these my little ones, you did unto Me." Echoing His sentiment the evangelist asks, "If you do not love your brother whom you see, how can you love God whom you do not see?" Vatican Council II saw in Jesus' teaching concerning love of neighbor "...a certain likeness between the union of the divine Persons, and in the union of God's sons in truth and charity."

The Christian bearer of the God-life is called to good works in service of his fellowmen for love of God. In its *Constitution on the Church in the Modern World*, the Fathers of Vatican Council II taught that "everyone must consider his every neighbor, without exception, as another self" and to do this in concrete actions of assistance, especially to those subjected to infirmities, oppression, privation, discrimination, and the like. Even one's enemies (echoing the admonition of Jesus) must be loved with the same holy love as are one's friends.

The Christian of every age has been called to the life of fraternal charity in and through Jesus; but this need is receiving, in our times, a renewed emphasis, and the new catechetics founds itself upon this Christian action as well as upon Christian beliefs. The gift of God-life will be stifled in a man indifferent to the needs of his neighbors—needs of truth, guidance, and understanding in religious matters, needs of individual and social human dignity in earthly values.

On the other hand, by witnessing the truth of Jesus and His Gospel to all men and by laboring to bring about social equality and justice for men of all races, economic levels, political systems and the like, the Christian increases and intensifies the God-life in his own soul. "Love your neighbor as yourself," when fulfilled in true brotherly service, is an imitation of Jesus and a positive, life-giving sign of fidelity to His covenant.

But the "social gospel" ought always to be a reflection of the salvific Gospel. The Catholic Church and its members work for the temporal good of every man and his societies as a work ultimately directed toward and in keeping with the Gospel message of salvation. Condemnation of evil and programs for betterment must be based on and reflect religious truth and values and lead toward religious ends.

If this distinction is not made, the Christian's basic role in the world—to be a witness to Jesus—will be destroyed. The politician, economist, sociologist have other objectives as their motivation in working for human betterment. The catechist's goal is and must be recognizable as the making of all things "new" in Jesus, and through Him bringing all men to the glory of heaven.

True service to mankind and to one's neighbor, as springing from and expressed in supernatural love, is today receiving recognition within a part of the Christian community in a new attitude toward pacifism and conscientious objection to warfare. This search for new insights has attained an extent and depth probably never before known in Christian history. In its *Pastoral Constitution on the Church in the Modern World*, Vatican Council II gave status, if not birth, to this reappraisal of Christian love in relation to military action. While presently the ranks of the theologically oriented pacifists number but a few and bear a blurred identity because of non-religious overtones and associations, continued study and discussion will undoubtedly increase those subscribing to pacifism to some degree or other; this, and the true relationship of pacifism and the commandment of love make mention of the movement appropriate to an orientation to new catechetics.

Just warfare, as an instrument of sovereign policy, has never been condemned as such by the biblical message nor the teaching Church. Indeed, the People of God in both the Old and New Covenants have used war as a tool in their survival and expansion kits.

Much of the investigation of the morality of warfare looks to the possibility whether, given present-day destructiveness of weapons, communications which intensify the oneness of all men, and diplomacy exercised within a family of nations, modern-day warfare allows for the label "just war" under any circumstances. True Christian pacifism (if such a thing feasibly exists), therefore, must not rest upon the negative foundation of "against war," but on the positive, Christian basis of the brotherhood of man which condemns Cain-like fratricide, on the command of Jesus to love neighbor and enemy alike, and on the promise of the beatitudes, "Happy are the peacemakers, they shall be called God's children."

But because authentic Christianity is a balanced way of life in which temporal realities are stepping stones to an eternal goal, the true exercise of the virtue of piety, which directs one to a love of country, and of prudence, which directs lesser acts to greater goods, cannot be set aside in order to develop a pacifist theology. As the Council Fathers point out, peace is not merely the absence of combat or a maintenance of national power blocs; rather, peace "...results from that harmony built into human society by its divine Founder and actualized by men as they thirst after ever greater justice." The fullness of the picture shows that defense of rights and the fulfillment of duties, due to the imperfect state of man's intellect, will, and concupiscence, may often require the exertion of righteous violence on behalf of international justice.

Vatican Council II, in the just-quoted *Constitution*, urges as pathways to securing peace with justice an abandonment of injustice and distrust between peoples and ideologies, cessation of the arms race, an international community for establishing and preserving peace among nations, multi-lateral disarming, and education-in-peacefulness for the masses. This same document, while recognizing and endorsing the deeper appreciation by individual consciences of the transcendent natural law and its principles, even to the point where conscientious objectors ought to be allowed to choose a non-combatant form of service to the human community in place of active military participation, yet also recognizes the legitimate right and duty of duly constituted government to pursue war when the means of peaceful settlement have been exhausted. It would seem that the Council Fathers would more direct anti-war sentiments in the direction of the mentioned antidotes to war in preference to a refusal to bear arms.

While consideration of the authenticity of Christian pacifism and conscientious objection to war will continue and increase, the catechist should bear in mind that the Church has not given definitive and unequivocal endorsement to a doctrine of non-war over just war. Catechesis can mention and explain the principles of pacifism and patriotism as Christian belief embraces both, but prudence will dictate identity of unqualified pacifism as a postulate derived from Christian principles, not as a Christian doctrine itself.

* * * * *

Sacraments, prayer, and fraternal charity bring about and/or increase the God-life in the earthly life of the righteous person. These are the positive, love-giving responses to the love God gratuitously extends to man. But man's response can also be in negative, love-refusing signs which lessen or completely destroy the God-life in his person. Man can act against divine love and indwelling, and such action is *sin*.

If the new insights into sacred doctrine and Scripture which modern study and research have brought about have caused a ripple upon the surface of religious tranquility, the current reappraisal of morality has been a tidal wave! Present-day catechetics finds its most formidable challenge in the area of contemporary versus traditional behavioral patterns and the modern psychological outlook and its reconciliation with morality as normally conceived While an in-depth study of this problem is beyond the objective of this book, certain basic considerations must be viewed to establish an orientation to morality as it is treated in the new catechetics.

Traditionally, sin was weighed against a set of laws or regulations either derived from the revealed will of God as expressed in Sacred Scripture or based on reason and the natural law as formulated by legitimate authority. The current theological approach to the problem of religiously unorthodox behavior increasingly tends to a concept of love response: the less response to God's goodness, the less love for God; and insofar as love is union, in a totally negative response, union is non-existent.

Both approaches, the conformity to law and the response-in-love, rest sin in the free will of man; the former is will choosing to accept or reject specific divine or ecclesiastical precepts, the latter is will reacting to the stimulus of God's goodness. In either case, sin as an act of free will conforms to the Genesis description given in the Eve-Adam confrontation with the tempter in which, after due reflection, a deliberate choice between alternatives was made. Either system of morality, then, makes sin an act of a human will. Both the "obedience to law" and the "response to love" explanation of sin also show that the human choice in question pertains to the man-to-God relationship. Generically, then, sin is described as pertaining to man's free choice or rejection of God manifested in very definite or specified ways of acting. And consequently, sin, potentially or actually, is a capability concomitant with achieving use of one's free will and not merely a question of a person's maturity.

Sin is the human will placing itself in opposition to the divine will, a rebellion on the part of man against God's creative and covenant plans for him. Sin is a rejection of the covenant fruits, and therefore a negative attitude of man toward God's call to adoption. Sin is an injury to the body of the People of God and, if the sin is also a crime, an injury to the body politic as well.

Since God is goodness itself, to the degree that a human choice rejects God it rejects goodness. Therefore, sin is a deliberate choice to do that which is known or believed to be partially or totally non-good or, the more common term, evil. A survey of the Old Testament evidence and an observation of human behavior patterns verify this definition.

Sin is a judgment by one's conscience to do the wrong ("ought not to do") rather than the right ("ought to do") in a human action pertaining to the moral order. Each person possesses the faculty of conscience and must guide himself by its dictates if he is to be true to himself immediately, and to God ultimately. In its *Declaration on Religious Freedom*, Vatican Council II emphasized this moral duty: "In all his activity a man is bound to follow his conscience faithfully in order that he may come to God, for whom he was created."

Conscience is the immediate or subjective norm of morality —good being what conscience demands, evil what it forbids. Consequently, each individual, because rational by nature and thus ordained to pursuit of the truth, necessarily is charged with the responsibility of having, as far as it is possible, a *true* conscience, that is, what subjectively is judged as "good" is really an objective good, and what is judged as an "evil" is actually a non-good. The same Council document just quoted also notes, ". . . every man has the duty . . . to seek the truth in matters religious, in order that he may with prudence form for himself right and true judgments of conscience."

Divine revelation provides the clearest objective standard for knowledge of the morally true and good, particularly in the "Ten Commandments" and in their fulfillment as enunciated by Jesus and recorded in the Gospel, and in the interpretations and applications of divine and ecclesiastical law made by the Catholic Church, Jesus' designated judge of eternal values. To the degree one is able, there exists the duty to know what God's revelation teaches about morality and the specific meaning which the Church attributes to revelation's content. The other side of the coin is the role of the Church as teacher and director of conscience. What is objective good and evil must be proclaimed to all, especially to those who act contrary to the objective norms, and most especially to the young whose consciences are in the early stages of formation. The Church would, indeed, abrogate one of its most essential roles were it to slight this area of teaching by allowing individual conscience to be misformed or to remain in an erroneous state. As a teacher, the Church is also and thereby a molder of conscience.

The present-day quest for this knowledge seeks also to obtain deeper insights into making morality more meaningful in the light of human psychology and responsibility. Closely related to the inquiry are the problems raised by the meaning of freedom and the applicability of situation ethics.

Freedom is the ability to fulfill the design inherent in nature (to be what a thing ought to be), thereby expressing existentially what a thing is essentially. In human freedom this resolves to being a creature in the image of God, capable of truth and goodness, possessor of the potential for infinity, and therefore destined to an eternity of truth and goodness. More simply stated, man is a creature made for union with God—imperfectly in this life (sanctifying grace) and perfectly after this life (beatific vision). Thus man is to have in the material order here on earth his due measure of recognition as the crown and master of subhuman creation, the opportunity to share in the goods of creation as these are developed by human ingenuity, and the dignity which is each man's as a child of God on pilgrimage to his Father's house. In the spiritual order, he is to have the message of the Gospel and the means of personal sanctification made available to him.

Briefly, man's freedom is the possession of happiness here on earth as a prelude to bliss in heaven.

True human freedom must recognize man as a temporal being born to a life on this earth and an immortal being ordained to unending union with God; a body bearing common traits with the animal kingdom, yet a soul which casts man in God's image; a distinctly individual person but at the same time a social being; at one and the same time the subject and the object of responsibility and authority. The comprehension and expression of freedom must be founded upon all of these facets. Thus freedom is not a right possessed by an elite or a privilege benignly bestowed on others by men or their societies, but rather is an inherent demand of nature placed there by the Designer of nature. Freedom is a duty of man, the duty to be *himself*—to satisfy the needs of body and spirit, subjecting the generically animal to the specifically rational; to reside in this temporal abode while yet preparing to live in an eternal dwelling; to exercise individuality of person in the framework of sociality of nature; to create and preserve the environment in which the fullest attainment of the human goals can be realized.

In His providence, God has made known the inner demands of man's nature by which he will fully and successfully express himself in true freedom—will really be himself. The law of man's nature is expressed in the Ten Commandments. Man's responsibility is to conform the subjective norm of his conscience to the objective norm which is this decalogue. When, and to the extent that, this identity is established and made the guide for life-situations, man will enjoy true freedom because by his positive, love-giving responses he will be moving along the way to God, the goal and purpose of his essence and his existence.

Freedom is expressed in two relational terms: responsibility and authority.

Precisely because a human being seeks freedom by the right and the forces of his nature, he must assume a position of responsibility within the community of men of which he is a part. Freedom is to "get" what human nature is owed and responsibility is to "give" what that nature offers. Responsibility to self calls for personal discipline and initiative in order that true and full human personality be developed; responsibility to society demands respect for the freedom of fellowmen and a contribution to the common good by necessary and communal restraints upon self.

Authority is a "must" for human life and organization. In the absence of effective authority, men tend to become less human. The jungle atmosphere of much of man's present-day world is created by a prevalent disregard for due authority.

Authority comes from God and unifies man, directing the many in pursuit of a single goal and giving identity and coherence to social actions. Parental, civil, ecclesial authority are direct extensions of divine authority; man's free associations (labor unions, lodges, protective associations and the like) are indirect extensions. Because of its divine origin and personal and social necessity, Christianity and its catechesis must incessantly uphold proper authority and promote and advocate respect for and submission to it.

The trend to reject authority in favor of that self-determination identified as "freedom of conscience" presents a serious challenge to Christian doctrine.

If the spirit of the new catechetics is to refind salvation within the solidarity of community—a "People of God," as was the concept in the Israel of old and the major part of the Christian era—emphasis on organization and objectivity in religious existence is proper, for these qualities are not contrary to community but are of its essence; and ordered social structure requires the authority of law and demands obedience to law as necessities of its life, for the absence of law and obedience is disorder, anarchy. A thriving People of God therefore supposes an objective legal base and a fidelity to lawful authority by all members. Abrogation of law is the introduction of lawlessness, and law is expressed in recognizable authority.

An appeal to objective community (the God-centered, peaceful assembly of the pre-sin Eden) and at the same time a demand for a subjective moral judgment which overrides both objective law and transcending authority (the self-centered turbulence of the Babel tower) is contradictory and self-defeating.

As was pointed out in our opening chapters, the new catechetics ought to be oriented to winning over the minds of the many as well as of the educated elite. The educated rightfully expect a religious presentation to exhibit the logical consistency these people find in the empirical fields of knowledge; the average man of the masses is blessed with a common sense that intuitively rejects incompatible propositions. A catechesis which hopes to be acceptable on the modern scene must therefore be faithful to one principle throughout: either the "People of God" idea with its objective norms of law, authority, and obedience or a "Liberty of Conscience" platform of subjective judgments and obedience of convenience. To try to teach both ideas in one and the same catechesis is to invite rejection in the judgments of intelligent people.

Contrary to some contemporary theories and practices, freedom, responsibility, and authority are not contradictory or contrary concepts. Rather, the three are complementary, to the extent that where one is stressed too much or toc little, the other two are damaged or destroyed.

The second basic point in determining man's proper choices in his moral behavior is the effect upon judgment of good and evil exerted by situation ethics (situationism, contectualism, etc.).

Christian doctrine proposes four considerations in the make-up of sin: the thing done or omitted, knowledge of doing and its consequences, the degree of free-will assent to the doing, and circumstances affecting the thing, knowledge, or assent. The simplest analysis of the various "situation ethics" systems of morality would seem to indicate that they judge morality by a part (circumstances) rather than by the whole (all four parts). In the non-religious (ethical) field the norm governing "to do or not to do" is the pragmatic, "does it work?" When situationism is applied in the religious (moral) area, the final judgment is determined by "love." Both procedures to some degree ignore any existence or reality to basic principles or to absolute, transcendent norms although, logically, the insistence upon individualism rather than objectivity as the norm of choice is itself an absolute principle.

Catholic moralists have not advocated an all-out religious theory or practice of situationism, and this for, at least, the very good reason that the teaching Church has condemned situation ethics as a norm of Catholic morality. But those theologians who attempt to find a reconciliation between authentic Christian moral teaching and situation ethics, or to see the former in the framework of the latter, seem to suppose an abrogation of law, a supersedence of law by love, or (in the general, cosmic upsurge way of thinking) morality as evolving from lower to higher forms. As shall be mentioned presently, divine or natural law was not abrogated but fulfilled in the evolution from old to new covenants, and love is not incompatible with law.

As to man and the cosmic upsurge, while man is a part of the created pattern, he is by his position of dominion a distinct and unique part to the extent that his basic natural norms are not made by the natures surrounding him, but rather man subjects subhuman creation to his own standards. In his moral realm, this human prerogative is formed and directed by revelation, not merely by human wisdom. The constancy and universality of God's word transcends the evolutionary and particular aspects of man's knowledge.

Yet the personal dynamism of man springing from his nature and so aptly expressed in love which is deepened by understanding cannot be meaningless in judging life-situations, nor must it blindly be totally subservient to an inflexible moral objectivity. The true approach to morality will come when the just demands of love and law are harmonized in the nature of man. Toward this harmonization Christian catechetics must continually strive in order to be true to itself and its goals. Law is not a ceiling upon Christian behavior but a floor under it; law is not the "way of life" but divinely given direction signs pointing out the way. The pitfalls presented by over-accenting either law or love need equally to be abandoned in favor of fidelity to the middle course which joins them. This merging of two facets will build the dynamically human super-structure of love upon the absolute foundation of law—a love modeled on law.

Love lifts man beyond himself, for it is a giving of self to the loved. And law, likewise, elevates man to where he sheds selfishness for the larger good of society. In this demand for giving of self, love finds a common ground with law. In turn, because of the divinely guaranteed teaching office of the Catholic Church, the absolutes of law which are proposed to the faithful rest on sufficient authority as to give full assurance and security to the one who follows them, and assurance and security are the foundations of love. Law and love are thus seen not as competitors but as complements.

Positive response to God's covenant will be motivated by love which is free because it sacrifices beyond the demands of law, not because it is destructive and contentious with it. But when and if God's Uncreated Love should fail to elicit a love-giving response from His creature, law and fear of sanctions can provide the motive for doing what man ought to do. Allegiance motivated only by law is still a positive response, for it is the practice of the virtue of obedience.

It would seem, then, that no true morality of human actions can rest solely on the circumstances of person, time, place, or the like. Morality requires more than a measuring stick of self-interpreted "practicality" or "love." "Situation ethics" treats only part of the question of sin. A full understanding and evaluation of human conduct requires consideration also of the action itself, the knowledge on the part of the doer, the degree of consent. In that total framework the true freedom of man and its consequent responsibility can be measured—not in mathematical or logical units but in degree of loving response to covenant living in the life-situations of time, in terms of intensity or absence of God-life in a human soul.

The Gospel records Jesus as teaching a positive, objective doctrine on sin.

The very beginning of Jesus' public ministry (after His confrontation with the devil in which the temptations of Eden were placed again but this time repulsed) proclaimed His messianic role by a call to repentance for sin. He announced that He had come to save that which was lost, that is, man lost to God through the separation of God and man brought about by sin; that He had come to cure the spiritual sickness caused by sin. In several parables Jesus taught of sin and its consequent debt, and of the mercy of God whereby due punishment was abrogated. Sin and its punishment even after death were several times mentioned in His teaching, and by physical

cures He symbolized the restoration to spiritual health concomitant upon the forgiveness of sin. Jesus urged the avoidance of sin as the formula for attaining heaven and urged men
to pray for divine forgiveness. Finally, He sent the Holy Spirit
to indict the world of its sin.

But most striking—and, indeed, sufficient unto itself—
was the new covenant between God and man which Jesus
brought about: announced at the Last Supper, accomplished on
Calvary, and certified by the empty tomb—"My blood of the
new and eternal covenant . . . shed . . . for the forgiveness of
sins." Sin must have been real in the value world of Jesus if
He paid such a ransom price to win men back from it!

The epistles of St. Paul make many references to sin and
sinful deeds, and much of the doctrine of these writings relates
to the subject of sinfulness versus justification, and of law
and liberty in the Christian evaluation of human acts.

Saints John, Peter, and James all develop to some extent
or other a moral theology based on the message Jesus transmitted to them, and the Apocalypse paints a vivid eschatological
picture of the victory over sin.

The Gospel and epistles of the New Testament report
also the need of repentance, and the ability of sincere contri-
tion to negate the deadening effects of sin. If a heart obdurate
against God's will separates man from God, drives out of the
human soul the gift of God-life, and renders impossible the
pre-ordained destiny to eternal union with God, so then does
this same heart reverse those evil effects when in sincere sorrow it turns back to God as Lord and Savior.

True Christian repentance for sin is not the repayment
of a debt but a changing of life-direction: turning back to
God and away from the sinful through faith in the healing
and saving message and power of Jesus. The measure of sin
and repentance is not quantitative but qualitative, not "how
much" but "how intense"—and such evaluations lead to full
positive response or total negative response with all the varying
shades between. Gospel morality, then, is to do the best one
is able in giving love to God for the love God gives to man.

*   *   *   *   *

The gift of God-life indwelling in a human person in his earthly life is a return to the primordial state of creation whereby man was not to die, but to live in unending union with God. Then not to die physically or spiritually; now to undergo bodily death as a sign of human sinfulness, but to live on spiritually and eternally.

At some point in time each person is to have his own "second coming" of Jesus. The Lord and he will meet to make life's most momentous decision—to live forever in the divine presence or separated from it. If by a life of positive love-responses man has preserved the presence of the Trinity in his soul, his eternity will be the perfection of that presence. If man should have made the life decision totally and irrevocably to bar the Trinity from his soul, this record of negative response will dictate an everlasting existence separated from the Godhead.

Only God knows how many billions of human persons have faced that moment of eternal truth wherein they saw themselves as they really were in the sight of God and made the final choice of will wherein their eternal destiny was determined. Only God knows how many more men are yet to come to the threshold of eternity. At the end of time, in a great manifestation of divine majesty and justice, all mankind will witness the glory of the saved and the ignominy of the lost. On that great day of judgment, each soul, glorified or damned, will again assume personal, bodily existence.

The Bible and the Church teach that of the earth's tenants who have departed, many have entered the presence of God or are in preparation to do so. In heaven there are the saints, those either publicly acknowledged in order to urge imitation of their example or whose names are known to God alone; awaiting heaven are the not yet perfectly cleansed; meanwhile on earth remain the pilgrims. These three groups constitute the redeemed of the Lord and form the communion of Saints. As in one body all members interact, so within the communion of Saints the glorified, the souls in purgatory, and the pilgrims on earth have oneness in praise and mutual interest.

That all the dead in Christ may appear undefiled in the presence of the heavenly Lamb and as members of His eternal court, the pilgrims on earth make restitution for sin by faith and by the practice of good works, particularly works designated by the Church for that purpose (indulgences); the faithful departed, temporarily sojourning in purgatory while awaiting triumphant entry into God's Presence, by their chastening period of expectation remove the final scars of the worldly journey.

Those who have ended the earthly sojourn divorced from faith in the saving power of Jesus and in sinful rebellion against the will of God for their salvation enter into everlasting hell to endure forever the torments of the damned. Hell is not a pleasant concept; it is difficult for the human mind to grasp its significance or to conceive its eternity. Yet the word of Jesus, statements in Sacred Scripture, and the teaching of the Church are unequivocal in asserting the reality of the state of the irrevocably lost.

The greatest danger to human souls could be wrought by a catechetics denying or temporizing the possibility of eternal existence in separation from God. In terms of the will of God that all men be saved, the redemptive covenant forged by Jesus for all mankind, and the limitations on human intellect and will by the state of sinfulness, the probability of eternal damnation may not be as great as that of salvation. No one knows the number of the saved; no one knows the number of the damned. This fact must always remain clear: God's covenant is a free gift which can be refused by the free will of man, and total refusal is total rejection of God—another way of saying hell!

At the end of the pilgrim's trail and after the final preparation in purgatory (should it be needed), the extended arms of the Father, the welcoming smile of Jesus, and the warmth of the Spirit's love will usher God's faithful child into the eternal homeland. The inheritance promised to the elect, the fraternity of the adopted, the reward of the faithful will be realized in a face-to-face encounter with God. The beauty of creation, the power of the universe, the peace of righteousness once enjoyed on earth, shadows that they are, will fade into nothingness by comparison to the reality who created them.

The exodus of man will have been completed and the Passover will have been fulfilled; the promised land at the end of the journey will have been reached. Man will have come to the destiny for which he was created, toward which the use of creation moved him, a preview of which God's indwelling gave him, in view of which salvation history was enacted, the accomplishment of which Jesus ordained in His own love and Blood. Man will be home—forever.

And at the end, the saved community of men, the redeemed People of God will be swept up into the perfection of the presence of divine goodness and love, to stand in the forever enduring moment of eternity as the completed tapestry of divine design, the full fruit of the redemption mystery.

Perhaps at the beginning God gave a picture of the end. The onrush into His heavenly arms will be with all the holy haste and ardor of Jacob leaving his earthly homeland to rush into the arms of his son Joseph—the distributor of life-giving gifts—there to find in a new land and full and plenty of a new life in joy.

Vatican Council II set the orientation for the new Christian catechetics. "... to set forth authentic teaching about divine revelation and about how it is handed on, so that by hearing the message of salvation the whole world may believe; by believing, it may hope; and by hoping, it may love." This book has read the Bible through the eyes of supernatural faith to discover that "authentic teaching."